(Opposite) A picture 'made up' as a Christmas greeting and photographed around 1929 at the bottom of Abington Street. *(Robert Wharton Collection)*

Another view of Abington Street in the mid-1930s looking towards Wood Street shows the shop frontage of Halford's, the well-known Northampton jewellers, and The Clarendon public house, much better known by its previous name of The Two Brewers, which would shortly be converted to a shop. *(Robert Wharton Collection)*

NORTHAMPTON
WELCOME TO THE PAST

PART TWO

People and Places

Frontispiece. Silver Street Nursery playground, on Thursday 6 June 1957, proving the old adage that 'it is not always the things that cost the most that give the most pleasure'. An old car body balanced on four tyres, some frayed rope and a few loose planks provide hours of fun – but what would today's Health and Safety Officer have to say about such enjoyable improvisation?

(Northampton Chronicle & Echo)

NORTHAMPTON

WELCOME TO THE PAST

—— *PART TWO* ——

People and Places

by

RICHARD COLEMAN and JOE RAJCZONEK

W.D. WHARTON

Wellingborough

First published in 1995 by
W.D. Wharton
37 Sheep Street
Wellingborough
Northamptonshire NN8 1BX

ISBN 0 9518557 8 6

Designed and typeset by John Hardaker, Wollaston, Northamptonshire
Printed and bound in Great Britain by
Butler & Tanner Ltd.
Frome, Somerset

ACKNOWLEDGEMENTS

Our sincere thanks are extended to the following people and organizations:

The unnamed photographers of both the *Northampton Chronicle & Echo* and Northampton Borough Council. Local photographers Les Hanson, Robin Puryer, Dave Rowe, C. Lucas, P. Rawlinson and P.H. Groom who have generously allowed us the use of their material, and John Meredith and Betty Davis, for the use of their fathers' negatives. Without all their marvellous pictures this book would not have been possible.

Northampton Mercury Co., in particular David Rowell, Editor-in-Chief, who gave us permission to use the *Chronicle & Echo* negative collection, and Trevor Cooper, the Librarian, who provided most useful information. Northampton Borough Council, especially Roger Morris, the Chief Executive and Town Clerk, who very kindly wrote the foreword to the book, and also to Bridget Peet and Sinead Ryan for the use of the Borough negatives. Northamptonshire Libraries, for giving us free access to the *Chronicle & Echo* negative collection.

Northampton artist Henry Bird, who kindly allowed us to use on the jacket flap a colour picture of his Sipario Dipinto from the Royal Theatre, and provided his own special recollections of Northampton in the past. Karla Dearsley, who interviewed Henry Bird and compiled his recollections. James Hollin, another Northampton artist, who so kindly gave permission for us to use his painting of the New Theatre to grace the jacket of this book.

Larry Byrne, from the British Gas Company in Northampton, for his enthusiastic response to our questions about the old gasworks. Nigel Lavender, Manager of the Royal Theatre, for supplying the transparency of the theatre's safety curtain. David Blagrove, for details about the canals in the Northampton area.

Special thanks to Mark Higlett, who coped admirably with our constant pressure to provide top quality handprints from the negatives provided for use in the book, and also to Jess Lay, for his remarkable retouching skills.

Finally, as always, our many thanks to the production team – John Hardaker for his continuing patience in face of our numerous requests to alter and amend our original layout and manuscript; Mick Sanders for answering our incessant questions about printing techniques; and finally Robert Wharton who has given us great freedom in the preparation of the book.

Half title caption
In recognition of Charles II's gift of timber to help the rebuilding of Northampton after the great fire in 1675, every year on Oak Apple Day (29 May) the verger of All Saints places an oak garland on the statue over the portico, seen here in 1966.
(Northampton Chronicle & Echo)

Title page caption
A pleasurable scene by the River Nene in the meadows adjacent to Kingsthorpe Mill as people make the most of a hot summer's day on Friday 29 August 1930.
(W.J.S. Meredith)

CONTENTS

FOREWORD

With my office in the Guildhall comes a magnificent and very large aerial photograph of the centre of Northampton. To me, who first came to the town only a decade ago, its date remained a mystery.

The authors of this book place it during the late summer of 1963. The Market Square fountain has gone (April 1962). The two blocks of flats in the Borough's area of the town have been completed (January 1963), but the electrification works to the railway in the vicinity of Castle Station have not yet started (May 1964). Suddenly the picture has acquired a further dimension.

The phenomenal growth of published pictorial records underlines not only the sense of nostalgia for apparently simpler times, but also the achievement of those who had the duty or the job to preserve these images in an era when the prevailing mood was very different.

While the photographers, in their pictures, capture a supposedly simpler way of life, they also often incidentally reveal all kinds of social realities and restrictions to which people today would not really want to return. For me, photographs of wartime and austerity years are particularly stark reminders of the sorts of tasks local councils faced, and of the armies of clerical and other labour necessary to carry through the measures people knew were necessary for survival. Above all, perhaps, such photographs show a community with an overwhelming sense of purpose, and a common spirit we may well envy.

We owe a debt to Richard Coleman and Joe Rajczonek for trawling these riches and selecting another group of the most memorable. They will allow us to clothe their pages with our own memories and impressions of the people and places they have chosen.

Who knows what riches remain to be found in the cupboards and attics of the town. Perhaps this collection will stimulate further discoveries which will foster an interest and pride in the traditions of Northampton which its newer citizens can never acquire from elsewhere.

Roger Morris
Chief Executive and Town Clerk
Northampton Borough Council

INTRODUCTION

In Part One of *Northampton: Welcome to the Past* attention was given to the changing face of the town predominantly during the era of the 1950s and 60s. Now, in Part Two, it is the turn of the people of the town to show what they did in their leisure time, the personalities who visited the town, and the many notable events that took place.

Children's Saturday morning cinema at the Gaumont or Savoy; watching the Cobblers play in the First Division at the County Ground; swimming at the open air pool at Midsummer Meadow; Saturday night dancing at the Salon, or going to a show at the New Theatre are just some of the aspects of Northampton life to be recalled.

Of the stars who came to the town, Laurel and Hardy, the Beatles, Roger Moore, Errol Flynn and Helen Shapiro are some who are featured, and local-bred names such as Judy Carne and Jackie Enfield are not forgotten.

Then there are those wonderful occasions, such as the Queen's coronation and Royal visits, the switching on of the town's Christmas lights and the famous carnival parade. The nostalgia continues with trips out into the county – to Billing Aquadrome, Towcester races and, of course, the Silverstone motor racing circuit in the days of Graham Hill and Stirling Moss.

This, without doubt, is a book that no true Northamptonian will wish to be without, with over 200 superb photographs specially chosen to convey the flavour of life in Northampton over 25 years ago.

Richard Coleman and Joe Rajczonek

HENRY BIRD REMINISCES ABOUT NORTHAMPTON

Henry Bird is still a working artist in the town at the age of 86. One of his finest achievements is the painting of the Royal Theatre's renowned Safety Curtain, still in use today, a picture of which appears on the front flap of the jacket to this book.

I was born in the Green Street area of Northampton near St Peter's Church in 1909. One of my earliest memories is of standing on a flat horse-truck next to my father's and uncle's stall just inside the fairground next to the cattle market, where they sold brandy snaps and confectionery when the fair was on. There were big crowds waiting for King George V and Queen Mary to drive past in a car on their tour to celebrate the Coronation, and I was disappointed they weren't wearing their crowns.

It was 23 September 1913. Cars were a rarity then, not a menace. Cattle were regularly driven through the streets to the market, and horses were everywhere; delivering coal, collecting rubbish, delivering milk – although in those days you took your jug and the milkman measured it from a churn; it didn't come in bottles. The car was special but, to me, Northampton has always been more important. Consequently, when I started travelling by rail to London on a regular basis at the age of about 15 to visit the Tate and National Galleries, after being awarded a prize by the Art School's Sketch Club (then in Abington Street), I could never understand why the Northampton train only went as far as Blisworth, where I had to change for Euston.

Later on, I discovered that I was not the only one who thought Northampton was special. Even in the Stone Age the place must have been significant, as a stone circle twice the size of the Market Square, which was unique in Britain, was built here (the last remains vanished when the Eastern District was developed). Geographically, politically and in religion the town has always been of central importance, which makes its bypass by the main railway line even more puzzling. Although I still cannot work out why the main line missed Northampton, I now realize that the results of this went far beyond a wait on Blisworth platform.

Northampton has always been full of character, and I do not just mean its buildings; there were some great individuals, too. One such was Ernie Fell. When I left school I worked for a while for Allchin, who made traction engines, then at Bell's factory. The fact that I shared an interest in drawing with one of the Board of Directors set me apart from the men. They saw me as different, and tried to put me off working there. When I returned from the Royal College of Art after virtually sweeping the board of prizes, I could not get work at all, so when signwriter Ernie Fell offered me work designing pub signs he was something of a saviour. His premises were in Newland – one of the many streets that have gone. He was an enthusiastic watercolourist and would go off to the country to paint landscapes whenever he had the chance. His priority was to find somewhere nice to sit, and if the view was not very good he would make it up. After lunch in a pub, Ernie would then find a nice quiet church to have a nap in.

In the fifties my old home disappeared under the bulldozer, which was pretty grim. No semblance of the cobbled area, known as 'the green', remained, nor of my grandfather's bakehouse, and all that replaced them was a muddle. But, by that time, I was living in Hardingstone, and it was still possible then to walk from the village into town across the fields and a country road to Nunn Mills. There was a level crossing on my route, with a gate for pedestrians. As I approached this one misty morning, I heard a train coming – a real train with a steam engine. Anyway, I could not see it and I was not in a hurry, so I leaned on the gate to wait for it to pass. Instead, the train drew to a halt and the engine loomed above me. A disembodied voice came down, saying: 'Come on, Henry, it's a long time since All Saints School', and the train waited for me to cross. All Saints was the school I attended before going on to Campbell Square School. I never did find out who the engine driver was, but that sort of thing would not happen now; not even for the Queen.

Sadly, both the fields and the characters like Ernie Fell have now gone, along with the confidence and daring that once put Northampton ahead of the rest of the country. In former centuries the town was at the forefront of trends in good architecture and technology, rather than just striving to be modern. Take the old flour mill which stood at the bottom of Tanner Street. In the nineteenth century it was converted into a cloth mill, weaving textiles by machine instead of by hand, before the great mechanized cloth mills were built in the north.

To our detriment, we also seem to have been at the forefront of the fad for demolition. The destruction of what remained of the castle to make way for the old railway station's goods yard in the last century was a foretaste of what has taken place since the sixties. Albion Place is an example. At one time this delightful row of Regency houses formed an elegant finale to the town opposite the cow meadows. First, the houses at the bottom were pushed down and replaced with an office block, then a big house with gardens all around which stood half-way down the street was demolished for a car park. Another marvellous building which was flattened to make way for the car was the St John's Street branch station at the bottom of Guildhall Road. This stood at a dead end, and the track skirted the meadows. The building was Victorian baroque with a big porch where the gentry could dismount from their carriages without getting wet if it was raining. Now, it's another car park.

If we had been on the main line, perhaps so much of the town would not have been given over to cars, but I think the most important consequence goes much deeper. Sometime this century Northampton stopped setting the pace and started to follow what was going on elsewhere. Local architects, artists, musicians and innovators are no longer valued by their fellow Northamptonians, even when they have gained international recognition. Is this because Northamptonians feel the cutting edge of culture and technology has passed them by along with the main track? It's time Northamptonians stopped regarding the town as being on the sidelines; it was, and still can be a very special place.

(Interviewed by Karla Dearsley)

NOTABLE EVENTS

1. Crowds have gathered on the Market Square and the route from the Town Hall as civic dignitaries head towards their seats in preparation for the 'Peace Parade' on the Saturday morning of 19 July 1919 to commemorate the ending of the First World War eight months previously. The Second Battalion of the Northamptonshire Regiment, known as the 'Steelbacks', are well to the fore, as are the 108 V.A.D. nurses present, better known as the 'Angels of Mercy' who, along with a number of young people's organizations, are all well turned out for the occasion. There would be mixed feelings amongst the people in the crowd, depending on whether their loved ones had returned home from the war or had been lost in action.

2. and 3. As the shadows lengthen, people gather on the Market Square on Thursday 23 January 1936 ready to hear the proclamation of King Edward VIII's accession to the throne. Little did the crowds realize that, with Edward's abdication after just 325 days, they would be gathering again less than a year later to hear the proclamation of King George VI. The memorial to Lt. Col. Edgar Mobbs, seen in the foreground, was moved later the same year to its present site on Abington Square. *(Both pictures: W.J.S. Meredith)*

4. For the Coronation of King George VI on 12 May 1937, three arches were erected as part of the town decorations. Here at the bottom of Bridge Street the second of the arches to be erected is prepared on Monday 3 May 1937. The arches were made by A. Glenn & Sons at their Kingsley works and cost around £100 each.

(W.J.S. Meredith)

5. Townsfolk in typical 1930s dress look on as the arch at the bottom of Bridge Street is erected later the same day. While under construction the columns had to be restrained at the top until the arch had been securely fixed in position. It required a team of 12 men to manhandle the arch into position, the total weight being around 2 tons. *(W.J.S. Meredith)*

6. The first arch to be erected was at the top of Abington Street on Thursday 29 April 1937, and here, amongst a wonderful array of vehicles, the final touches are being put to the arch with the fixing of Union Jacks and bunting. To the left of the arch can be seen the huge picture of the future King and Queen fixed to the front of the Savoy cinema.

(W.J.S. Meredith)

7. The third arch was at Black Lion Hill, photographed on Coronation Day, Wednesday 12 May 1937, just as people are gathering for the forthcoming coronation parade through the streets of the town. The unusually-shaped stone building on the left stands on the corner of Black Lion Hill and St Andrews Road, surviving until the late 1950s before the inevitable demolition. *(J. Davis)*

8. Just as All Saints' clock strikes 12 noon, people gather at the top of Gold Street ready for the Coronation Day parade through the streets of the town on Wednesday 12 May 1937. The day was proclaimed a national holiday, unfortunately not applying to public transport workers or the policeman standing in his traffic control point. The people's clothing is typical of the 1930s period.

(J. Davis)

9. A glance round the corner from the previous picture finds The Drapery festooned with flags and bunting in this busy lunchtime scene on Coronation Day. During Sunday 9 May wind and rain had played havoc with the decorations, blowing over one of the standards outside All Saints, necessitating some urgent remedial works. It is a sign of the times that H. Samuel were proclaiming themselves to be 'The Empire's largest jewellers'.

(J. Davis)

10. The Northampton Co-operative Society frontage in Abington Street, elaborately decorated for the coronation on 12 May 1937. With Coronation Day fast approaching, a sticker on the window advertises decorations at 'cost price'.

(J. Davis)

11. Although the decorations are up, Abington Street appears rather subdued on the dull Sunday of 9 May 1937 in this view looking from the town centre towards Fish Street. Happily, by Coronation Day on the 12th there was great jubilation in the town, with streets and buildings a mass of colour and the local population making merry. *(J. Davis)*

12. Abington Street from Wellington Street looking towards Abington Square on Saturday 8 May 1937, and people seem in the mood to decorate everything ready for the coronation on the following Wednesday, right down to the front of bicycles and jacket buttonholes. *(W.J.S. Meredith)*

13. The Coronation Day parade which toured around the streets of the town consisted of some 50 lorries and floats. The 'Roadmender Boys Club' brings up the rear of the parade, turning into Overstone Road from The Mounts on 12 May 1937.

(W.J.S. Meredith)

14. Around 300 streets in Northampton were decorated for the May 1937 coronation, and the Mayor and Mayoress, Alderman and Mrs G.W. Beattie, toured 250 of them during the day. Here we look down Regent Street from Regent Square as the residents make preparations for their celebrations. At the end of the street can be seen St Andrew's Church, later to be demolished during August 1972. *(J. Davis)*

RICHMOND · TERRACE
LITTLE BUT LOYAL

15. Richmond Terrace was probably the smallest street in the town to celebrate King George VI's coronation, consisting of only nine houses, but the residents put on a splendid display of decorations. A tea party, followed by sports, was planned for Coronation Day afternoon, and refreshments would be provided during the musical and communal celebrations, during which a collection would be made for Northampton General Hospital.

(J. Davis)

16. King George VI's Coronation Day, 12 May 1937, and in Alma Street, St James, the street tea party is under way with the children all enjoying themselves, except perhaps for the lad pulling faces on the right of the picture. Most street parties started at 4 p.m. and the sun was still shining, but soon after it started raining, and by 7 p.m. it had become a torrential downpour, flooding the streets – with puddles tinted red and blue by the dye that had run from the soaked bunting – and completely spoiling the later outdoor celebrations.

(W.J.S. Meredith)

17. At Alma Street, earlier in the day than in the previous photograph, the tables are all set up and laid ready for the afternoon party. The list of celebrations was to include sending up balloons, a bus ride for the children, tea, sports, singing and dancing, refreshments and a collection for Northampton General Hospital. The total number to be entertained was 160, of whom 42 were children.

(W.J.S. Meredith)

18. Even the fountain on the Market Square was dressed up for the coronation of King George VI in May 1937, and here we see four young ladies passing the fountain on 12 May while out celebrating along with the other townsfolk. Earlier in the day a divine service was held on the Market Square, transforming the square from a centre of trade to a great open-air cathedral.

(W.J.S. Meredith)

19. As part of the town celebrations to mark the coronation of King George VI in May 1937 a number of buildings in the town were floodlit. According to the *Chronicle & Echo*, the Town Hall looked particularly impressive, lit from the buildings on the opposite side of St Giles Square, especially as the areas each side of the main entrance steps had been filled with flowers. In this 11 p.m. view, one of Guildhall Road's gaslamps makes a brave attempt to compete as it casts its ghostly shadow on the road and pavement below.

(Les Hanson)

20. 'Long Live The Queen' as the decorations go up again in readiness for the coronation of Queen Elizabeth II on Tuesday 2 June 1953, with the *Chronicle & Echo* offices and the Emporium Arcade putting on a particularly impressive display at the top of the Market Square. Around the square flagpoles have been specially erected for the occasion, flying the flags of different countries within the Commonwealth. Flags and bunting are also in evidence along Newland where preparations are being made to extend the *Chronicle & Echo* building.   (*Northampton Chronicle & Echo*)

21. A view from Wood Hill on to the Market Square, showing the street decorations for the coronation of Queen Elizabeth II in June 1953, for which a colour scheme of red and yellow was used. At the bottom of the Market Square can be seen the specially erected 'bell tower', but overall the decorations appeared rather subdued in comparison with those for the 1937 coronation. It was at this time that the street gaslamps in the central area were being removed and replaced by electric fluorescent lights, both types being on view here. *(Northampton Chronicle & Echo)*

22. The procession arrives at the Market Square, with the Mayor, Alderman W.A. Pickering, and the Corporation followed by a contingent from the Northamptonshire Regiment and other local organizations in readiness for the divine service at 10 a.m. to commemorate the coronation of Queen Elizabeth II on Tuesday 2 June 1953. A closer view of the bell tower reveals a dove of peace perched on the tower, with imitation bells and bell ringers within, under which were loudspeakers broadcasting a recording of bells being rung. *(Northampton Chronicle & Echo)*

23. Trying their best to ignore the rain, civic dignitaries await the forces parade march past, due after the divine service on Market Square, to commemorate the coronation of Queen Elizabeth II on Tuesday 2 June 1953. At the front of the podium Deputy Mayor, Alderman Percy Adams, waits to take the salute. *(Northampton Chronicle & Echo)*

24. and 25. In many Northampton factories the workers put up decorations in the weeks before the coronation of Queen Elizabeth II. Here we see two very happy groups of workers posing for the *Chronicle & Echo* photographer, no doubt looking forward to the extra day's holiday. The gatherings are at Parker and Tearl shoe factory on The Mounts (above) and Crockett and Jones shoe factory in Perry Street (opposite). *(Northampton Chronicle & Echo)*

26. and 27. It is Thursday 8 July 1965 and Her Majesty Queen Elizabeth II visits Northampton for the first time as the reigning monarch. She arrived at Kettering station mid-morning with the Duke of Edinburgh, and after visits to Kettering, Higham Ferrers and Wellingborough she lunched at the Guildhall in Northampton. The photograph above shows the Queen preparing to leave the Guildhall surrounded by local dignitaries and press photographers. Her next appointment was at Church's factory in St James, and she is seen opposite waving to the crowds as her Rolls Royce travels along Marefair. Many people had gathered along the route to catch a glimpse of the Queen, and this remarkable photograph shows her in a relaxed and happy mood. Later, the Queen travelled to Althorp to visit Earl Spencer, and finally departed from Sywell Airport at tea time.

(Above: Northampton Chronicle & Echo. Opposite: Robin Puryer)

28. Many notable events pictured in this section have occurred within the area covered by this impressive aerial photograph taken over the town centre on a late summer Saturday in 1963. This is one of a number of aerial photographs in the book where we have chosen a place or building from a 'bird's-eye view' and compared with a photograph at ground level.

(Northampton Borough Council Archive)

29. Back to ground level and it's the last day of Regiment Week on Sunday 2 July 1950, and the Duchess of Gloucester has just placed a wreath on the Cenotaph in the grounds of All Saints Church. Standing beside the Duchess is General G. St G. Robinson of the Northamptonshire Regiment, while behind him the Regimental buglers prepare to sound 'The Last Post' followed by 'Reveille'. *(Northampton Chronicle & Echo)*

30. Members of the 1st Battalion of the Northamptonshire Regiment find time to relax while waiting for their train at Castle Station on Monday 14 July 1958. Having taken part in 'Exercise Steelback' in the Northampton area, they are returning to their barracks at Oakhampton. Try as we may, we have not been able to identify the lady with sunglasses being escorted down the platform.

(Northampton Chronicle & Echo)

31. On Thursday 17 October 1935 a locomotive of the 'Royal Scot' class No. 6147 was named 'THE NORTHAMPTONSHIRE REGIMENT' by Lady Knox in a ceremony at Castle Station. The footplate crew, consisting of driver George Quartermain and fireman Duff, were both ex-Northamptonshire Regiment men, and here we see the highly polished and decorated locomotive moving down platform 1 to take up its position in readiness for the naming ceremony. *(W.J.S. Meredith)*

Inset: THE NORTHAMPTONSHIRE REGIMENT nameplate and badge as fixed to 6147.

32. (above) and 33. (inset opposite) Northampton Castle Station plays host to a Stephenson Locomotive Society special on Saturday 14 April 1962. The tour originating from Birmingham travelled a total of 240 miles, calling at Northampton, Bedford, Hitchin, Hertford North, Welwyn Garden City, Hatfield, Luton, Dunstable, Leighton Buzzard, Weedon and Leamington Spa. It arrived at the station at 12.10 p.m. behind one of the last surviving Fowler 2P 4-4-0s No. 40646, and became the centre of attraction as much clicking of camera shutters was performed by the travelling enthusiasts. In fact, the railway had to come to a halt as some of the 330 passengers swarmed on to the tracks under West Bridge to photograph the train from various angles. After the line had been blocked for some 10 minutes an irate BR official herded them back to the train, muttering 'Are you all trying to commit suicide?' His reaction is not surprising when you look at the various positions the enthusiasts have placed themselves in. On the left-hand side of the photograph, the grey-haired gentleman next to the post is Arthur Camwell, a well-known figure amongst railway enthusiasts, renowned for his cine films from the days of steam.

(Both pictures: Northampton Chronicle & Echo)

34. Members of the local Railway Correspondence and Travel Society mingle with fellow railway enthusiasts on Saturday 25 August 1962 at Northampton Castle Station in the company of Fowler class 4P locomotive No. 42350. It was the occasion of the Fernie Rail Tour, the last to be organized by the Northampton Branch of the RCTS and the first to start from Northampton Castle Station. The itinerary was arranged to travel along many of the branch lines of Northamptonshire, and the train travelled via Market Harborough, Seaton, Uppingham, Peterborough, Luffenham, Manton, Oakham, Kettering, Thrapston Midland, Wellingborough, Higham Ferrers and back to Northampton via the Bedford to Northampton route. John Mawby, on the locomotive (far left) and Keith Locke (the Chairman of the Rail Tour Committee) standing next to him – the organizers of the tour – pose for photographs before the departure.
(Northampton Chronicle & Echo)

35. At Northampton's Memorial Square, situated off St Katherine's Street, on Saturday 17 May 1952, Professor Frank Dobson is bathed in sunshine as he addresses the gathering at the unveiling of his statue 'Woman with Fish'. He may well have been explaining the reasoning behind his choice of subject – something to do with the idea that life originated in the sea..

(Northampton Chronicle & Echo)

36. The 'Woman with Fish' statue was much ridiculed over the years, being daubed with paint on more than one occasion, and eventually losing her head. After the decapitation, gardener Bill Packe retrieves the pieces for safe keeping on Monday 1 March 1965. The statue was removed and taken into storage, during which time the head was repaired, and thereafter was resited in Delapre Park. *(Northampton Chronicle & Echo)*

37. An aerial photograph in the vicinity of Abington Square on Friday 22 July 1966. The shops facing the camera on Kettering Road, and the area behind up to the Wellingborough Road were all demolished over the years, and a new housing estate subsequently erected. At this time all but two of the properties on the left-hand side of Wellingborough Road up to St Edmund's Hospital had been demolished ready for road widening. St Edmund's Church, opposite the hospital, would survive until 1980 when it was demolished, leaving only the churchyard.

(Northampton Chronicle & Echo)

38. On Friday 6 November 1959 two elephants and their handlers from Roberts Brothers' Circus toured the town collecting money for World Refugee Year. The statue of Charles Bradlaugh on Abington Square points them in the direction of the town centre as they make their way towards the Town Hall. Behind Charles Bradlaugh on Kettering Road is Wareings slipper factory, another building that would be a casualty of the town's modernization. *(Northampton Chronicle & Echo)*

39. A pleasing spectacle in Northampton on Friday 26 April 1968 was the visit to the town of the Watney Red Rover stagecoach and four, here passing All Saints on its way from the Yeoman of England at Wootton to the Town Hall – a reminder of times gone by when this form of transport was looked upon as the norm and could have been seen in this locality making for the Peacock Hotel on Market Square. *(Northampton Chronicle & Echo)*

40. The elephants seen in picture 38 arrive in front of the Town Hall on Friday 6 November 1959, and are met by the Mayor and Mayoress, Councillor and Mrs George Nutt, who are there to receive the collecting tins for World Refugee Year. Rebecca stands quietly with the Lady Mayoress, but Baby (the large elephant) provides cause for laughter with her wandering trunk. *(Northampton Chronicle & Echo)*

In Town Tonight

41. (opposite) and 42. (above) Two tremendous views of Market Square at night, photographed on Thursday 26 September 1963 at 8.40 p.m. The collection of parked vehicles is a quite outstanding reminder of the types of cars in general use at that time. To support the national Civil Defence publicity campaign, the Northampton Civil Defence Corps, with the Women's Voluntary Service, the Auxiliary Fire Service and the Special Constabulary were staging a demonstration of vehicles and equipment from 2 p.m. to 9 p.m. on this day (seen opposite near the *Chronicle & Echo* building). Notice also the intriguing view up the deserted Newland in the right-hand corner of the picture opposite. A sad sight is the stump of the once famous fountain which occupied pride of place in Market Square until being needlessly demolished in April 1962. With only a small number of people visiting the exhibition one wonders where the occupants of all the cars are spending their evening. No doubt many were in the Gaumont cinema where *The Great Escape*, starring Steve McQueen, was being shown for the second week. An Oscar Wilde play at the Repertory Theatre will also have been a draw, and the rest were probably enjoying a drink or two in The Queen's Arms or The Admiral Rodney, both of which can be seen in the picture above. *(Both pictures: Northampton Borough Council)*

43. Northampton voters turn out in force on Market Square to listen to the Labour and Conservative candidates for Northampton on Wednesday 7 October 1959, the eve of a General Election. In this view Mr Paget, the Labour candidate, is in forceful action talking to some 300 people, a number which had almost doubled by the time Mrs Jill Knight arrived. Soon, derisive cheers and boos from the Conservative ranks mingled with counter cheers and clapping from the Labour supporters. Mrs Knight's speech, subject to much hostile barracking from Labour, lasted 24 minutes compared to Mr Paget's 42 minute oration. The following day the Northampton poll was a record 83 per cent, and Mr Paget triumphed over Mrs Knight by a majority of 2,700 votes, although nationwide the Conservative Party were the overall victors. Mr R.T. Paget (later Lord Paget) was Northampton's MP from 1945 to 1974.

(Northampton Chronicle & Echo)

44. A group of traders in Abington Street took a huge gamble in 1959 when they purchased 121 lanterns and 3,000 fairy lights from Regent Street in London at a cost of £5,000 to illuminate Abington Street and Square over the Christmas period, the first time such a scheme had been tried in Northampton. Crowds were out in force for the 'switch on' on Friday 20 November 1959 as a Chronicle & Echo photographer freezes a moment in time with the assistance of a super flash gun at the lower end of Abington Street.

(Northampton Chronicle & Echo)

45. Film star Shirley Ann Field is guest of honour at the Christmas light switch-on ceremony on Friday 18 November 1960. She had arrived earlier in the day to visit two children's homes and Church's factory in St James, and later went to the Gaumont cinema. Over 5,000 local people came to see her, and the switch-on ceremony in the Boots arcade was a success. As the buglers of the Royal Pioneer Corps sounded a fanfare, Miss Field flicked the switch and the chandeliers of Gold Street burst into colourful light. The chandeliers were the Christmas decorations in Regent Street, London, the previous year. On the platform with Miss Field are Councillor George Nutt (Deputy Mayor), on her right, and Mr Graham Jelley, the chairman of the Gold Street Traders' Association, on her left.

(Northampton Chronicle & Echo)

46. A quite outstanding view down Gold Street – the narrowest of Northampton's shopping thoroughfares – the day after the annual Christmas lights had been switched on on Tuesday 16 November 1961. The previous evening, film star Jacqueline Jones, the guest of honour, had attracted a huge crowd of about 2,000 local people who were lined up, ten deep in places. The Gold Street Traders Association had organized the whole event, and Gold Street was transformed into a corridor of glitter and gaiety as Jacqueline Jones switched on the six huge chandeliers, with over 1,200 multi-coloured lights, slung 50 ft. high on tubular steel arches. Once again Gold Street lived up to its ambitious claim to be the brightest shopping street in the country outside London!

(Northampton Chronicle & Echo)

47. It is Christmas lights switch-on time on Friday 20 November 1959, and crowds throng Abington Square and Abington Street to watch the magnificent Christmas decorations, consisting of coloured lanterns and a myriad fairy lights. The event was always well attended, and the organizers always attempted to make Abington Street 'the most beautifully lit street in the Midlands'. Many Northamptonians will no doubt remember those happy days when all the family would go to the town to cheer and whistle at the great moment when the lights were switched on! On this occasion, the Mayor of Northampton, Councillor George Nutt, performed the duty.

(Northampton Chronicle & Echo)

48. A twilight look down Abington Street on Monday 28 November 1960, showing the Christmas lights shining brightly. The lights were first switched on on Friday 25 November but, because of heavy rain, there were few spectators to witness the event. During the Christmas period the lights were automatically switched on every day from mid-afternoon to 11.30 p.m. The Notre Dame School buildings can clearly be seen on the right-hand side of the picture. *(Northampton Chronicle & Echo)*

49. A very appropriate guest of honour at the Repertory Theatre's 75th birthday production of *Twelfth Night* was actress Fay Compton, seen leaving the theatre in Guildhall Road after the first performance on Tuesday 5 May 1959. It was Fay Compton's father Edward who appeared in the theatre's first production of Shakespeare's *Twelfth Night* to mark its opening as the 'Royal Theatre and Opera House' on 5 May 1884. Currently known as the Royal Theatre, great entertainment can still be found within its wonderfully chandeliered Victorian auditorium.

(Northampton Chronicle & Echo)

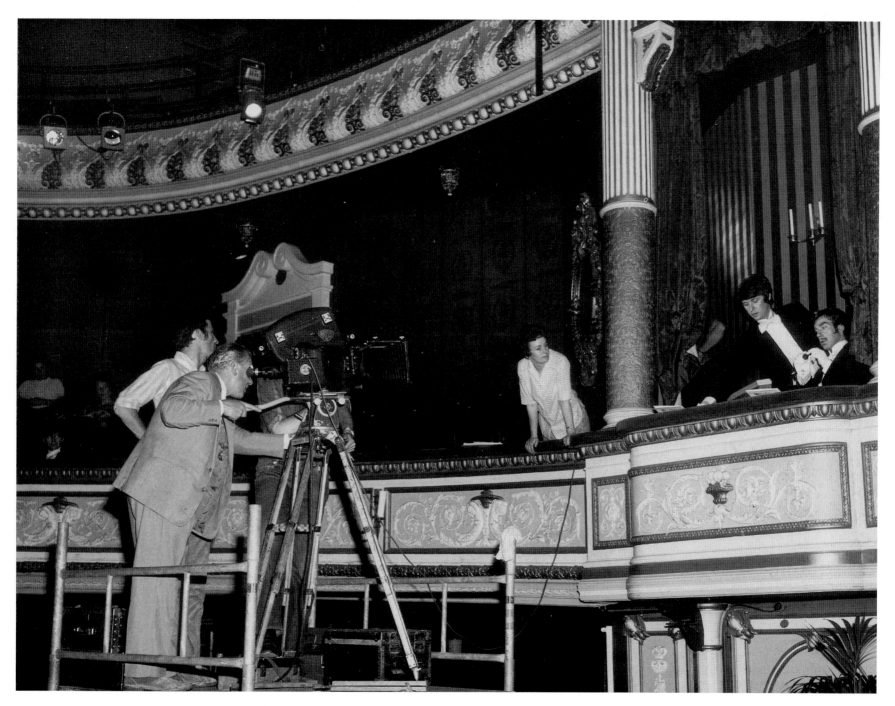

50. On Monday 1 July 1968 a BBC film crew make preparations at the Repertory Theatre to shoot scenes for Emile Zola's *Nana*, a new television series that was to be shown in August of that year. *Nana* is based on a factual story of how a girl took Parisian theatre by storm in the 1880s, and it was felt by the TV producers that Northampton's Repertory Theatre was the most authentic setting. Unfortunately, the coach bringing the actors and actresses from London was held up for three hours by an accident on the M1, putting filming at the 'Rep' well behind schedule.

(Northampton Chronicle & Echo)

51. At one time it was the 'in thing' to go out ballroom dancing on a Saturday night, and one of the most popular places in Northampton was the Salon Ballroom at Franklin's Gardens. It was at the Salon that you could dance to the big-band sounds of Eric Law and Art Lewis amongst others, with occasional visits from the likes of Joe Loss or Victor Sylvester. In this view, so typical of the Salon, the dance floor is packed with people enjoying themselves on Christmas Eve, Friday 24 December 1965.

(Northampton Chronicle & Echo)

52. The Salon Ballroom (originally called 'The Salon-de-danse') was often used for special functions such as the Art Revel Ball, seen here on Tuesday 12 December 1961. In this photograph the students are really into the swing of things, as Susan Seward (left) and Suzanne Duprée, dressed as a couple of exotic birds, launch themselves into the air while dancing with a tribal-looking Ian Stephen. *(Northampton Chronicle & Echo)*

53. (above) and 54. (opposite) A dancing establishment that became synonymous with Rock and Roll and Jiving was 'Gayeways', situated off Abington Street and run by Jean Smith and Ron Stanley. Pupils from the Gayeway School of Dancing are seen here on Monday 10 November 1958 during a break at the refreshment bar and (opposite) jiving the night away in the dance hall. The premises were eventually closed for dancing, and converted into a restaurant. *(Both pictures: Northampton Chronicle & Echo)*

55. Thursday 28 January 1960 was the night that traditional jazz enthusiasts in the Northampton and surrounding area had been looking forward to for some time – the opening of the new jazz club at the Embassy Ballroom in Gold Street. Many great names in traditional jazz were to appear at the Embassy, starting with Ken Colyer's Jazzmen, seen here in full swing in front of the 300 strong first night audience. *(Northampton Chronicle & Echo)*

56. The entrance fee to the Embassy Jazz Club was 5s (or 4s for members) whether you wished to sit at the front and listen or dance in the area to the rear of the ballroom. The recognized dance to traditional jazz is called 'The Stomp' or 'Stomping' and here we see two girls (one almost disappearing in the haze as she swirls around) dancing barefoot on Thursday 6 September 1962 to Ken Colyer's Jazzmen in the smoky atmosphere so typical of the Embassy. *(Northampton Chronicle & Echo)*

57. Crazes come and go, and one such craze during the 1950s was attending dances dressed in pyjamas. On Thursday 9 January 1958 Jackie Bates (left), Janet Smith and Glenda Wherry attend one such function in the Whyte Melville Hall, St Giles Street. For the time of year it is hoped the girls arrived at the hall in warmer attire, although some of the lads at the dance would no doubt come out with witicisms about 'warming them up'.

(Northampton Chronicle & Echo)

58. A 'lovely legs' competition with a difference at the Fanciers' Working Men's Club in Wood Street on Tuesday 4 February 1958. The event was organized by a local dancing club, inspired by the film *Les Girls* then showing at the Savoy cinema. Three girl judges represented the Savoy, the judge studying form in the picture being Dawn Brown. Quite what the lads were doing above the screen is not known, but they seem to be enjoying themselves. *(Northampton Chronicle & Echo)*

59. One of the most well-known local groups during the 1950s was the Apex Skiffle Group who played at a number of local venues, even managing to play on stage at the New Theatre, topping the bill and filling the house on 4 August 1958, just 12 days before the theatre's final performance. They were also National Skiffle Champions and Radio Luxembourg Skiffle Champions during that year. The group, from left to right, Roy Horn, Tom Dawkins, Colin York, Frank (Curly) Short and Ian Patterson, are going through their routine at the Black Lion Inn, St Giles Street, on Monday 22 December 1958. Ian Patterson changed his name to Ian Hunter and became part of Mott the Hoople, and is now a star in America. *(Northampton Chronicle & Echo)*

60. The Grand Hall in the Guildhall was frequently used for a variety of events during the 1950s and 60s. Here, it was the venue for a 'Youth for Christ' rally on Saturday 14 January 1967 which was attended by some 550 young people. The Hall was decorated with cardboard spiders and rope netting and, just for the evening, took the name of 'The Web Coffee Bar'.

The jazz band is the Don Clarke Jazzmen from London, who played several traditional jazz favourites in authentic style. In between the numbers the members of the band discussed the reason why they themselves were Christians. *(Northampton Chronicle & Echo)*

61. What an amazing collection of scooters, 'bubble' cars and mopeds can be seen in this photograph taken on Saturday 20 February 1960, the first day of the motor show organized by Mr Andre Baldet. Earlier, the Mayor of Northampton, Councillor George Nutt, opened Northampton's third motor show at the Town Hall, after officially declaring open the new premises of Moto Baldet Ltd. in the Campbell Square. At the time, several new models of mopeds and scooters were on display offering the prospective customer a wide choice.

(Northampton Chronicle & Echo)

62. An autumn fashion show organized by Adnitts of Northampton is in full swing at the Town Hall on Tuesday 29 September 1967. Two shows were put on, one in the afternoon and one in the evening, with nearly 2,000 people attending. Six models displaying a wide range of clothes (ranging from those for the shorter woman to the fuller figure) brought a splash of colour and luxury to the parades. For the fashion experts, the model in the photograph is wearing a cape made in fine soft leather with a zip up to the chin and slant pockets. At the time this garment from the Cresta range was priced at 22 guineas (£23.10). *(Northampton Chronicle & Echo)*

63. (left) Bonfire night on Wednesday 5 November 1958 and the youngsters are out on the streets having a good time and in some cases generally causing havoc. The young couple embracing seem oblivious to what's going on around them, but they are about to get a sudden shock as a 'banger' fizzes on the pavement not two feet away. The culprits are caught in the act by the photographer's flash gun as the leader backs away with another 'banger' still in his hand.

(Northampton Chronicle & Echo)

64. (opposite) Being out on the town at night was not always linked to pleasure, as we see at Marefair on Monday 2 January 1967 where firemen fight a fire in the upper floors of the Marefair Social Club. On the ground floor a light dimly shines through the smoke swirling around within the building.

(Northampton Chronicle & Echo)

VISITING CELEBRITIES

65. From 19 to 24 October 1953 famous slapstick comedians Stan Laurel (the thin one) and Oliver Hardy were appearing in a show at the New Theatre in Abington Street, their first time on stage in this country since returning from California. While in town they presented autographed story books to the winners of an art competition organized by the *Mercury &* *Herald* Merry Comrades Circle. The competition was to draw a picture of Laurel and Hardy. After watching the show at the New Theatre, the winners were taken backstage by 'Auntie Dick' and are seen here receiving their prizes. *(Northampton Chronicle & Echo)*

66. The appearance of Laurel and Hardy at the New Theatre happened to coincide with 'Car Safety Week' between 19 and 24 October 1953, so the duo agreed to give the cause some extra publicity. Here, in Abington Street at the entrance to Albert Place, the comedians perform with a vintage 1902 Wolseley, entertaining the crowd in their efforts to get the message across. *(Northampton Chronicle & Echo)*

67. Probably remembered most as a television personality, especially for his commentaries during the great Royal and State occasions, Richard Dimbleby was also a well-known radio broadcaster. On Monday 28 and Tuesday 29 April 1952 he was in Northampton recording an edition of Down Your Way and, after interviewing some of his guests, he relaxes at the rear of the Town Hall by signing autographs for a group of young admirers. *(Northampton Chronicle & Echo)*

68. Stanley Baker watches with interest as a young lady machines uppers during his guided tour of Manfields shoe factory in Wellingborough Road on Thursday 7 November 1957. At the end of the tour he was presented with a pair of hand-made shoes. The actor was in Northampton as the Guest of Honour at the annual Cinema Ball held at the Salon Ballroom the previous evening. *(Northampton Chronicle & Echo)*

69. Bertram Mills Circus's world-famous Coco the Clown made a point of having his special boots checked whenever the circus came to Northampton. They were made at Stricklands in Clare Street, and he is seen having his badges as well as his boots examined at the factory on Tuesday 2 April 1957. On this occasion, however, Coco's size 28 boots are dwarfed by the size 74 boot in the foreground which had been made by the company for advertising purposes. *(Northampton Chronicle & Echo)*

70. While performing in Northampton, people from the circus invariably paid a visit to the local hospitals in an effort to cheer up the patients, especially the children. At Northampton General Hospital on Tuesday 2 April 1957 Coco the Clown signs a few autographs as he entertains the patients. He was also a great advocate of road safety, hence his Belisha beacon walking stick with its flashing top. Coco's real name was Nicolai Polakovs, and when he retired from circus life he decided to settle in the village of Woodnewton near Oundle, where he is now buried.

(Northampton Chronicle & Echo)

71. A popular singing group closely associated with Northampton was the Beverley Sisters. During the war the three sisters were evacuated to the town from London. The twins Babs and Teddie worked for the *Chronicle & Echo*, while sister Joy became a private secretary for a local businessman. It was from Northampton that they appeared with the 'Blitzcoveries' concert party entertaining the troops, which in turn led to their first week's music hall engagement at the Croydon Empire in August 1945. The Beverley Sisters soon reached the top of the variety ladder both in Britain and America, appearing on various television and radio programmes, and cutting disks such as *Teasin'*. Here, on Tuesday 16 August 1951, the sisters inspect a new Russon lightweight tourer at Newland Motors garage near the Market Square. The car was reported to have a 250 cc engine with a cruising speed of between 35 and 45 m.p.h. and fuel consumption of 60 to 70 miles per gallon. *(Northampton Chronicle & Echo)*

72. The famous film star Shirley Ann Field arrives at Castle Station on Friday 18 November 1960 for a nine-hour visit to the town. Her main reason for coming to the town was to switch on the Christmas lights, but she also appeared at the Gaumont cinema, and made visits to the Dr Barnado's Home in Dallington and the St James factory of Church and Co. Ltd. She won the hearts of the many Northampton people who came to catch a glimpse of her, and she accepted the invitation to become the first President of the Gold Street Traders' Association – the group who organized the Christmas lights in Gold Street.

(Northampton Chronicle & Echo)

73. A youthful looking Roger Moore, star of *The Saint* series on TV, is surrounded by many admirers before opening a £4,000 show house, built by Wilsons on the Abington Vale estate in Northampton, on Saturday 24 November 1962. He was besieged by about 200 autograph hunters as he came out of the house, and his signature was nearly always accompanied by the matchstick man with halo *Saint* motif. He was later to become a famous film star, particularly in his role as James Bond.

(Northampton Chronicle & Echo)

74. At Sywell Aerodrome on Sunday 27 June 1954, film star Errol Flynn and his then wife, Patrice Wymore, prepare to board a Consul aircraft for their flight back to Croydon, near London. To see them off is stage and screen actress Freda Jackson, wife of local artist Henry Bird. Errol Flynn was in Northampton to appear with Freda Jackson at a fête held in Franklin's Gardens in aid of the Little Theatre Building Fund. It was the first time the two stars had met since they both appeared at the town's Repertory Theatre 20 years previously.   *(Northampton Chronicle & Echo)*

75. Denys Watkins-Pitchford attends a signing session at R.S. Savage's bookshop in Kettering Road on Monday 23 October 1967 to coincide with the publication of his book *Summer on the Nene*. Better known as the author 'BB', Denys Watkins-Pitchford was born in Northamptonshire in 1905, where he lived for most of his life, writing more than 60 books which he illustrated himself. He also illustrated 35 books for other authors, as well as contributing articles to countless magazines. His writing was mainly of the British countryside and its wildlife, his portrayal and perception of which gained him the reputation of the greatest lyrical writer on the countryside this century, for which he was awarded the MBE in 1989. He also wrote a number of children's books, and *Little Grey Men* won him the Carnegie Medal in 1942. His *Brendon Chase* was made into a television series.

(*Northampton Chronicle & Echo*)

76. Popular Scottish broadcaster and TV personality Fyfe Robertson interviews a Mr W. Hammersley by the fountain in Market Square on Thursday 2 June 1960 for the following week's *Tonight* programme screened by BBC TV. The question he was asking local residents was: 'If Hercules could be brought to Northampton today, what 12 labours would you give him? Fyfe apparently received some rather unusual answers and a lot of blank looks. *(Northampton Chronicle & Echo)*

Wednesday 6 November 1963 was an important night in Northampton's entertainment history, for it was on this night that the Mersey beat came to town in the shape of the most famous of all Liverpool groups, the *Beatles*, who played on stage at the ABC cinema.

77. (right) Heavy rain kept would-be sightseers away from the first house, but between 200 and 300 fans without tickets turned up hoping to catch a glimpse of the group leaving the cinema after the second house. Some of the fans are seen here in jovial mood at the bottom of Lower Mounts. *(Northampton Chronicle & Echo)*

78. (left) There were two performances with 2,000 people at each house. Here we see some of the satisfied customers leaving the cinema after the second house and heading for home with their souvenir programmes.

(Northampton Chronicle & Echo)

79. The Beatles, dressed in smart grey suits and winkle-picker shoes, go through their routine on the stage of the ABC cinema . The collarless jackets were a trademark of the group and were very much in fashion at the time. Gelgray's clothes shop in Northampton was selling collarless jackets at £4.19s.6d. each, and a suit with collarless jacket could be purchased for £9.19s.6d *(Northampton Chronicle & Echo)*

80. The supporting acts appearing with the Beatles were Peter Jay and the Jaywalkers, the Vernon Girls, Brook Brothers and the Rhythm and Blues Quartet. According to the *Chronicle & Echo* reporter, Peter Jay and the Jaywalkers put on a very polished performance and their fans seemed less than impressed by the Beatles or their screaming followers.

(Northampton Chronicle & Echo)

81. During the Beatles' performances their music was drowned by the screaming of the fans who, with flailing arms and eyes glazed with adulation, became caught up with the mass hysteria of the event.

'Beatlemania' had come to the town! The young ladies in this photograph were oblivious of the presence of the photographer.

(Northampton Chronicle & Echo)

82. John, Paul, George and Ringo on stage at the ABC cinema on 6 November 1963 beginning the first of their 10 numbers which would culminate with 'Twist and Shout' during 26 minutes of mass frenzy. Items thrown on to the stage during the performances included autograph books, panties, a girdle, flowers – even money – as the fans' excitement reached fever pitch. That they could not hear the music for screaming was irrelevant, they could listen to that at any time on their record players.

(Northampton Chronicle & Echo)

83. Privileged staff at the ABC cinema obtain the Beatles' autographs soon after the group had arrived for their two performances on 6 November 1963. Elaborate plans had to be made for the group's getaway after the second performance. While the National Anthem played, the Beatles made their way under police escort across the car park at the rear of the cinema and through a factory into St Michael's Road where a car was waiting to speed them away to safety and the M1 back to London. In the meantime a decoy coach with the supporting acts left the ABC car park entrance in Lower Mounts and was mobbed by the delirious fans.

(Northampton Chronicle & Echo)

84. Heady days at the County Ground, as the Cobblers are in Division I of the Football League for the first time in their history! The first home game on 25 August 1965 against Arsenal ended in a 1-1 draw. The second home game, three days later, was against the mighty Manchester United, and the photograph shows the world-famous footballing legend Denis Law leading his team out on to the field. Over 21,000 supporters, at the time the largest League gate ever at the county ground, watched the match, and it could have been more had the date not clashed with the local British Timken show. In the end, Manchester United were lucky to go home with a 1-1 draw after the Cobblers, with their superior fitness and enthusiasm, had dominated the match. *(Northampton Chronicle & Echo)*

85. (above) Local swimming star 15-year-old Jackie Enfield has her pulse taken after a last training swim at the Mounts Baths on Friday 9 November 1962 prior to leaving for the VII British Empire and Commonwealth Games in Perth, Western Australia, where she was to compete in the 220 yards breaststroke. *(Northampton Chronicle & Echo)*

86. (right) Jackie Enfield returned from Australia having won a silver medal in the breaststroke, and is seen here showing it to 16-year-old singing star Helen Shapiro on Thursday 13 December 1962. Helen was in Northampton performing on stage at the ABC cinema with co-stars Eden Kane and ventriloquist Arthur Worsley with his dummy Charlie Brown. *(Northampton Chronicle & Echo)*

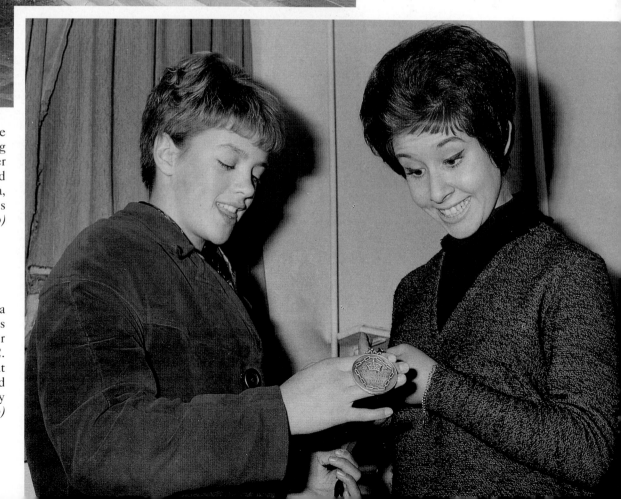

87. A blanket awaits a huge pile of coins pushed over the counter at the Old Five Bells public house in Kingsthorpe on Monday 17 March 1969 by TV star Judy Carne. The cash, made up of pennies (old 1d pieces), had been given by customers in aid of the Beacon Fund for Spastics. The coins amounted to over £31. Judy Carne, whose real name was Joyce Botterill, lived in Northampton and attended the local Pitt-Draffen Dancing Academy before becoming a TV actress and moving to Hollywood. She starred in a TV series called *Fair Exchange* and later married film actor Burt Reynolds. *(Northampton Chronicle & Echo)*

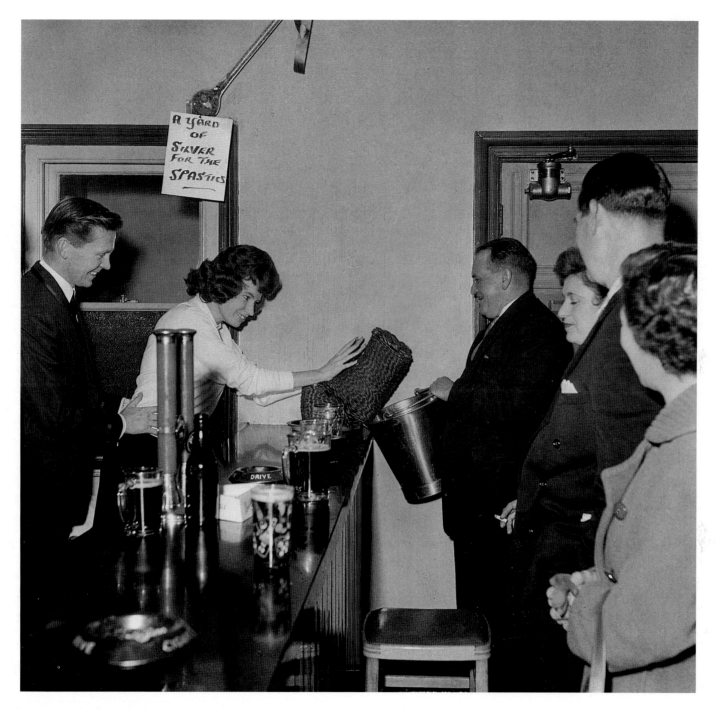

88. In between her many singing appointments, Ruby Murray takes time out to attend a function at The Cock Hotel in Northampton on 27 October 1961, also in aid of the Beacon Fund for Spastics. She is seen pushing over a pile of pennies into a bucket before pouring silver coins out of the 'yard of ale' which can be seen above her head. She is accompanied by her Northampton-born husband Bernard Burgess, one-time stage hand at the New Theatre. On this occasion the coins amounted to over £60. Ruby Murray will be remembered for her singing success in the 1950s, and at one time had five hits in the Top 20 chart – a feat which not even Elvis or The Beatles were able to achieve! *(Northampton Chronicle & Echo)*

89. THE DAWN OF A CAREER – Margaret White nonchalantly makes up in the mirror at the Denise Pitt-Drafen Dancing Academy on Wednesday 21 January 1959. After three years training at the academy, Margaret took her first steps to stardom by winning a place in the West End musical *Blue Magic* with Shirley Bassey, followed by a trip to Paris with the Charley Ballet and eventually joining the famous Bluebell Girls. Moving across the Atlantic, Margaret joined the Las Vegas Bluebell Girls appearing in Stardust Hotel's 'Lido de Paris Show' and was named 'International Showgirl of the Year for 1968', a title that promised a role in a 20th Century Fox movie. *(Northampton Chronicle & Echo)*

90. THE TWILIGHT OF A CAREER – Bertha Willmott makes up in the mirror of the No. 1 dressing room of the New Theatre over a year after its closure on Tuesday 8 September 1959 as she recaptures for a moment the atmosphere that used to be present in the 'top of the bill' dressing room. A singing star of the Music Hall, Bertha first appeared on the New Theatre stage in 1932 at the bottom of the bill, but topped the bill on her very next appearance, gaining a place in the No. 1 dressing room. Many times Bertha returned, topping the bill with the famous names of variety, and she could remember the days when the theatre was so full, people stood alongside the stall seats to make sure they did not miss the show. Then there were the broadcasts, for Bertha Willmott was known as 'Radio's Bright Star' performing in at least three *Henry Hall's Guest Nights* from the New Theatre stage. Bertha and her husband, Reg Seymour, were also proprietors of various hostelries, which included the Spinney Hill Hotel in Northampton and The Galleon at Wolverton. *(Northampton Chronicle & Echo)*

91. Another picture of the Beverley Sisters, one of Britain's top close-harmony trios during the mid-1940s and 1950s, who were topping the bill with Jack Jackson at the New Theatre during the third week in October 1951. During that week, on the very foggy morning of Tuesday 16 October, twins Babs and Teddie (left) and Joy climb aboard a Nortax taxi for a local shopping tour. These shopping tours were arranged for various stars appearing at the New Theatre, often attracting large crowds and a lot of publicity for local businesses.   (*Northampton Chronicle & Echo*)

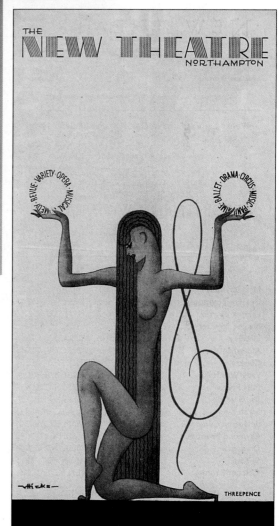

92. (above) The New Theatre in Abington Street opened on Monday 9 December 1912, and closed after the last performance on Saturday 16 August 1958, in between which many famous stars trod its boards, including George Robey, Gracie Fields, Laurel and Hardy, Rex Harrison, Norman Wisdom and Frankie Vaughan, to name but a few. The twenties saw many highlights in the theatre's glittering career, with queues stretching from the booking office into Abington Street and round into St Giles Terrace where people waiting to go in collected autographs from the artistes as they entered the stage door. Sadly, in later years the size of audiences dwindled and ultimately resulted in closure. It is seen here on Monday 23 February 1959, waiting for inevitable demolition.   (*Northampton Chronicle & Echo*)

93. (right) The New Theatre used various designs on its programmes during the 46 years of entertaining the people of Northamptonshire. This Art Nouveau design used during the mid-1940s was quite eye-catching, being printed in different shades of grey on a cream background, with the treble clef and the figure's lips picked out in red. This particular programme for the week beginning Monday 14 August 1944 listed famous actress Anna Neagle starring in a production of Jane Austen's *Emma*.

(*R. Coleman collection*)

94. At the New Theatre on Thursday 17 September 1959 the audience take their seats for the last performance in the 1,513-seater auditorium designed so that no pillars obstructed a view of the stage. The performers are the auctioneers from Jackson Stops and Staff who were about to sell the contents of the theatre prior to demolition. Incidentally, 100 stall seats were sold to the Gayeway Dancing organization at 7s.6d. each. Another 300-odd seats went to the Coventry Opera House at 15s each. The programme, for years sold at 3d, had gone up to 1s and the contents were not half as interesting. *(Northampton Chronicle & Echo)*

95. Looking past the plaster hanging down from the ceiling of the New Theatre, we see the painting over the proscenium arch that was soon to be smashed to pieces with the start of demolition in January 1960, removing yet another part of Northampton's history. *(Northampton Chronicle & Echo)*

TRANQUIL MOMENTS

96. This scene could be deep in the heart of the country, but in fact it is at Kingsthorpe only about two miles from Northampton's town centre. People stroll along Mill Lane on Sunday 17 May 1964 enjoying the peaceful surroundings and glorious weather in the days when little use was made of this road access between Kingsthorpe and King's Heath. How things were to change in years to come, especially for the folk who lived in Kingsthorpe village who would lose their tranquil country lane.

(Robin Puryer)

97. The familiar spire of Kingsthorpe Church overlooks this delightfully rural scene by the banks of the River Nene in Mill Lane, Kingsthorpe, on Wednesday 19 July 1967. For many years a location where youngsters have spent many happy hours swimming, fishing and having a good time. On this occasion, although the school holidays are just about to begin, a class of schoolchildren are fortunate to be spending an afternoon out of school, messing about by the river. With so little traffic using the road they can enjoy themselves without the worry of being disturbed in this tranquil area of the town.

(Northampton Chronicle & Echo)

98. This wonderful picture of a little boy being inquisitive is splendidly captured by the photographer at the Northampton Ram Fair, being held at the Cattle Market in Northampton on Saturday 19 September 1959. As the auction of rams and lambs takes place, the little fellow is obviously very keen to see what all the fuss is about! A picture that many of us see from time to time, but find it so difficult to actually capture on film.

(Northampton Chronicle & Echo)

99. The men of the Inkerman Company of the Grenadier Guards staged a recruiting drive in the town on Wednesday 26 September 1962. They performed sentry duties at designated points in the town, and one of these was outside All Saints Church. Many townsfolk came to admire the smart-looking guardsmen dressed in their colourful uniforms. Here, two very young children inspect guardsman John Turland, himself a Northamptonian, who stands perfectly still. *(Northampton Chronicle & Echo)*

100. This was the view along Victoria Promenade on Monday 17 March 1947. The River Nene was in flood, and water had spread across the Cattle Market (in the background) and the surrounding area. The flood, amongst the worst in the town, resulted from a rapid thaw of very deep snow following one of the most severe winters on record. One wonders whether the three schoolchildren waving from their 'island' were carried out to the seat for the photograph. Their shoes don't look wet, so it's unlikely they waded out themselves.

(Northampton Chronicle & Echo)

101. A party of schoolchildren from a nearby school, all neat and tidy in their uniforms, cross a winter wonderland in Abington Park on the morning of Wednesday 5 December 1962. For four days, a blanket of freezing fog had hung over the scene, but on this fifth morning the winter sun was beginning to make an impression, and as the fog cleared it revealed a frost-encrusted scene – the sort that makes for those unique winter photographs if you are able to get out with your camera before the ice starts to melt.

(Northampton Chronicle & Echo)

102. Autumn has arrived at Abington Park. The morning sunshine beams through the remains of the early morning mist as a road sweeper performs his solitary duties on Wednesday 26 October 1966 in this atmospheric picture of another rural area of the town. Park Avenue South is remarkably quiet and almost free of cars.

(Northampton Chronicle & Echo)

103. Once again the winter weather extends its grip on the town, and 12° of hard frost and thick freezing fog has transformed even the most ordinary objects into things of great beauty. Hoar frost of the last two days has coated all the branches of the trees in the grounds of Delapre Abbey on Wednesday 15 January 1959. The dramatic silhouette of the gentleman leaning against the tree and standing against the wall of fog further enhances the picture. Take him away and the picture would look lifeless! *(Northampton Chronicle & Echo)*

104. A peaceful winter scene in the grounds of the Church of the Holy Sepulchre photographed on Monday 13 January 1964. A pedestrian walks along the path whilst snow clings to the railings, roofs and trees to create a pattern of winter elegance. This tranquil scene is almost timeless as some 850 winters had already been seen by the church by this time, and no doubt many thousands of local folk have used the same path over the centuries. The church remains one of only four round churches left in England, and is probably the largest and best preserved.

(Northampton Chronicle & Echo)

105. A tranquil moment near the town centre in the garden of Vigo House off the Bedford Road on Wednesday 28 January 1959 looking across the front of the house to Vigo Mill. This ancient mill, seen here converted to living accommodation, was constructed and used in connection with a scheme to pump water into the town from 1722 to 1753. As long ago as the nineteenth century, ornamental lakes in the grounds of the house were illuminated at night, creating a very impressive and unusual sight for the 1800s. Sadly, both house and mill have since been demolished.
(Northampton Chronicle & Echo)

106. A peaceful scene in Abington Park on Sunday 5 August 1962. The annual art exhibition is taking place opposite Abington Park Museum showing the work of many local artists. From its first season in 1961, the exhibition proved to be very popular, attracting between 100,000 and 200,000 visitors each year. The venue later changed to the Central Museum in Guildhall Road, but in 1995 was back in Abington Park in the courtyard of the Museum. *(Northampton Chronicle & Echo)*

107. People gather around the bandstand in Abington Park on Saturday 14 May 1960 to watch the May Dance Festival presented by the Northampton Square Dance Society. As many as 60 dancers took part, a lot of whom were Society members, and they were dressed in a variety of costumes ranging from the bells and braces of the Northampton Morris Men to the kilts of the Scottish dancers. The music was provided by the Country Dance Band led by Miss Nan Fleming Williams. Some nine years earlier the Society decided they would like to revive interest in country dancing in the Northampton area, and at the time they hoped to make a tradition of their May Festival in Abington Park. When the Park opened to the public in 1897 the bandstand was a celebrated venue for many of the leading bands in the county, and attracted huge crowds for concerts. It is pleasing to note that bands still play, although the crowds have reduced in size. *(Northampton Chronicle & Echo)*

108. An idyllic setting on the platform of Northampton Bridge Street station in the days when station staff were given the opportunity to take pride in their station surroundings. Porter J.G. Law is seen tending the roses, the garden's speciality, on Monday 11 September 1961. The other gardeners amongst the station staff included porter E. Watts and clerk W.F. Withams, and they had just won the coveted title of the Best Kept Station Garden competition in the Rugby District. This was quite a feat in the days when many other stations in the local area were competing. The station had also won the competition in 1956 and 1957, so this gave them a hat-trick.

(Northampton Chronicle & Echo)

109. The use of a telephoto lens for this photograph, taken from West Bridge on Monday 27 March 1961, has allowed a most unusual view of the platforms at the north end of Northampton Castle station. The rural scene shows part of Northampton No. 2 signalbox and a class 4F locomotive shunting in the yard, whilst in the foreground a house and garden in Parkwood Street are prominent. *(Northampton Chronicle & Echo)*

110. It is a few minutes before 10 p.m. on the evening of 7 June 1963, and the photographer has ventured down to Mill Lane to find that after a fine hot summer's day, the cool evening air has caused a sea of mist to form in the valley below. The distant spire of Kingsthorpe Church contrasts with the set of semaphore signals which control the passage of trains through this part of town. A remarkable image, and no doubt very nostalgic for those who lived in the King's Heath and Kingsthorpe area of the town.

(Robin Puryer)

111. A tranquil moment as railway workers relax and sit down for a cup of tea and a chat in between their work levelling ballast and dismantling floodlights in the tunnel at Kilsby on Thursday 29 October 1953. It was the final day of repairs in the 2,500-yard-long tunnel which had been closed since 28 September. Northampton railway enthusiasts would really have enjoyed this period of time, as all the main line trains were diverted via the town. Incredibly, the work in the tunnel was done both day and night, and it was finished right on schedule! Within a few hours this peaceful scene would be replaced by the passage of steam trains creating their own smoke screens.

(Northampton Chronicle & Echo)

112. A nostalgic look up Newland at the end of December 1938 in a scene that simply oozes with the atmosphere of the 1930s. Not a car in sight: the bicycle providing the mode of everyday personal transport, and the horse and cart still used to move materials. The two workmen on the *Chronicle & Echo* building take a break to pose for the camera, and below them the hoarding displays a wonderful set of posters. *(Northampton Chronicle & Echo)*

113. A peaceful scene at Cotton End Wharf on Tuesday 5 May 1964 with one of Northampton's well-known landmarks in the background – the former Crown maltings which were built in 1877. Former bargee, George Beechey, lock-keeper on the Northampton arm of the canal, performs one of his main jobs – keeping the 17 locks free from rubbish. He uses a keb, a 20 ft.-long pole with a large rake on the end, and finds the most precarious part of the operation is cycling along the road from his home in Blisworth carrying the pole over his shoulder! Born and bred alongside the canal he spent the first 60 years of his life on the narrow boats before moving into the lock-keeper's cottage at Blisworth with his wife.

(Northampton Chronicle & Echo)

114. An artistic view of Cotton End Wharf on Monday 23 March 1964 showing a number of narrow-boats moored in company with a disgruntled boatman. Following heavy rain, the water in the River Nene between Northampton and Wellingborough had risen to about 12 in. above the normal level, and consequently proved to be too high for boat navigation. This caused 14 boats carrying grain from London to Wellingborough to become stranded at Cotton End Wharf. The first pair of boats had already been stationary for a week, and the boatmen were marooned until later the following week when the water level dropped sufficiently to enable them to continue their journey. *(Northampton Chronicle & Echo)*

115. The end of the road for freight traffic on the Northampton arm of the River Nene. The photograph shows a pair of narrow boats moored at Cotton End Wharf, having just made their last trip to Wellingborough carrying grain on Wednesday 2 April 1969. The firm that had kept alive commercial carrying on the Arm, Willow Wren Canal Transport Services Ltd., had been carrying grain to the Wellingborough mills of Whitworths Holdings Ltd. for over 20 years. The journey took the narrow boats from Blisworth to Northampton along the canal arm and then along the River Nene to Wellingborough. Alas, a new grain terminal at Tilbury Docks meant it was to become more economical to bring the grain in by rail, and hence the end of an era of narrow boat freight traffic through the town.

(Northampton Chronicle & Echo)

116. A peaceful scene from South Bridge overlooking the River Nene as the sun sets following a splendid day on Friday 5 September 1969. On the right the building of wine merchants Brown & Pank still stands proud next to the old coal gas retort house which had been superseded by the new gasworks in the background. All looks quiet in the vicinity of the gasworks as the summer shutdown period continues to the end of the month.

(Northampton Chronicle & Echo)

117. A dramatic picture of Northampton gasworks at night, on Monday 9 January 1967, reflected in the River Nene near South Bridge. At the time the gasworks was still under construction, with only one of the four re-forming plants (gas-making streams) actually commissioned and under test. By the end of the year all four were in full commission. Construction began in 1965, and the works was at the time the first of its kind in the county to use the Topsøe process of re-forming gas, a Danish invention. The total area covered by the Northampton works was about 34 acres, and the plant remained in operation for about another three years before closure. In 1973 the plant was demolished – a Northampton landmark that only survived some eight years! *(Northampton Chronicle & Echo)*

118. The peace of early morning at Hunsbury Hill is disturbed by the herald blowing on his horn to welcome the sun as it rises over the Northampton skyline at 4.40 a.m. on Sunday 20 June 1965. The Druids are celebrating the 'Sunrise Ceremony' of the summer solstice, looking out over the site of an ancient stone circle, the evidence of which was discovered by archaeologists working for the Development Corporation. A further ceremony was enacted at noon when the 'Lady of Alban Hervin' offered the 'Horn of Plenty' to the Chief Druid.

(Northampton Chronicle & Echo)

119. On the beautiful summer's day of Wednesday 29 June 1960 in the peaceful grounds of the Roman Catholic Cathedral in Barrack Road, four nuns contemplate the crucifix while holding an outdoor service surrounded by the wonders of nature.

(Northampton Chronicle & Echo)

120. (above) and 121. (opposite) Two peaceful scenes inside the chapel to the Convent and Notre Dame High School in Abington Street on Wednesday 29 March 1967 during an open day. The flashlight shows to good effect the ornate craftsmanship on the altars in the main Sacrarium (above) and the Lady Chapel (opposite). It all looks so permanent, but on a Sunday morning in April 1979 bulldozers ripped the building apart, reducing this fine chapel to a heap of rubble, from which would rise mundane-looking commercial and office buildings. Fortunately, some of the items in these photographs were portable and transferred elsewhere prior to demolition. *(Both pictures: Northampton Chronicle & Echo)*

122. No-one in sight in this external view of the chapel at Notre Dame on a February day in 1971 which shows the adjacent grounds and garden to the rear which extended right through to Lady's Lane – an oasis in the heart of busy Northampton. Built in 1881 and demolished in 1979, the chapel was used by the Nuns of the Convent and the pupils and staff of Notre Dame School. All that remains now is a small Convent graveyard situated adjacent to the footpath in the hustle and bustle of Notre Dame Mews, instead of the peace and tranquillity it once enjoyed.

(Northampton Chronicle & Echo)

123. (right) and 124. (below) The Notre Dame High School building dominated the north side of Abington Street for nearly 100 years, and in these two views taken to the west in 1913 (right) and to the east on Monday 17 February 1964 (below) very little has changed apart from the removal of tram tracks and wires. The view would change dramatically in the mid-1970s, however, when the bulldozers moved in and removed the school from the Northampton landscape. The need to expand the girls school and also to provide an upper school for the boys was the reason for moving to the new Thomas Becket Roman Catholic Upper School at Parklands.

(123. Robert Wharton collection)
(124. Northampton Chronicle & Echo)

PLEASURABLE PURSUITS

125. What a way to start the week at school – going to the pictures! It is Monday 31 January 1966 and children from various county schools pack into the ABC cinema for a film show and talk on road safety. It is interesting to see the concentration on most of the children's faces, although the little chap in the foreground has found it all too much and has nodded off to sleep, probably recovering from his weekend at home!

(Northampton Chronicle & Echo)

126. (left) No videos in the 1950s and 60s to keep people at home; consequently going to the 'pictures' was a regular pastime for many, and for the children Saturday morning cinema was very much a treat every week. When Walt Disney's first full-length cartoon film *Snow-white and the Seven Dwarfs* was shown for the first time in Northampton at the end of February 1965 it proved to be very popular. A queue of mums, dads and their children stretches from the Odeon cinema all the way along the Parade to Newland on Saturday 27 February 1965. The Odeon first opened as the Exchange cinema in 1920, became the Gaumont in 1950, was renamed the Odeon in 1964 and the last film was shown on 7 September 1974.

(*Northampton Chronicle & Echo*)

127. (right) Hordes of jostling fans converge on the doors of the ABC cinema at 10 a.m. to buy tickets for the forthcoming 'package' rock show featuring Del Shannon, the Shangri-Las and Wayne Fontana and the Mindbenders on Saturday 13 February 1965. Incredibly, some had queued since 1 p.m. the previous day (21 hours earlier), and about 30 had slept on the pavement overnight, to make certain of obtaining their tickets!

(*Northampton Chronicle & Echo*)

128. Can this really be a boat outside the ABC cinema advertising the film Watch Your Stern on Wednesday 30 November 1960? It is in fact a boat built on to a lorry frame, complete with number plate! Certainly a novel way of promoting the film and catching the eye of potential cinema customers. Incidentally, many of the stars in this film made the *Carry On* films such a success at the time. Sadly, the ABC cinema closed in 1995. It was the last of the 11 cinemas that were in business during the early 1950s in Northampton. *(Northampton Chronicle & Echo)*

129. This incredible sight outside the Cinema-de-Luxe in Campbell Street on 18 October 1930 predates the previous picture by 30 years, and clearly set the precedent for this form of film promotion! 'Cardinal Wolsey' gazes down in astonishment from the Wolsey underwear poster at this means of advertising the film *All Quiet On the Western Front*, while the girl on the weighing machine is less impressed. The Cinema de Luxe, which opened in 1911, had space for up to 1,000 people, and continued in business until the late 1950s.

(*W.J.S. Meredith*)

130. A light-hearted moment on the Racecourse as children on their summer holidays have fun and games on one of the damaged park benches on Thursday 13 August 1959. At the time, gangs of Teddy boys roamed the Racecourse at night, and vandalized the seats, breaking the slats in a show of so-called strength! Although the seats make fine playthings for the youngsters, they are of little use to the older generation who visit the Park. Alas, this form of vandalism is still an everyday occurrence.

(Northampton Chronicle & Echo)

131. With temperatures in the mid-70s and the school holidays in full swing, mums and their children flock to the play area known as 'Happy Valley' at Abington Park on Monday 22 July 1968. A popular spot where mums can chat and watch over their children, who make the most of the sand pit where the inevitable sandcastles are built and then crushed. Who needs the seaside when there is sand available in the Park. No doubt the three boys in the foreground are contemplating what game to play next! Generations of children had played in the same area for some 70 years before this picture was taken, and continue to do so. This is one part of Northampton which, it is hoped, will remain untouched.

(Northampton Chronicle & Echo)

132. Abington Park in the sunshine viewed from the air on Friday 22 July 1966 showing the lakes, water tower and golf course, all very familiar sights at ground level but not often seen from a bird's-eye view. Fortunately this area of town has changed very little over the years, and many people will have taken a Sunday afternoon walk in the Park, and children will have been 'bandy netting' for fish or have taken out a paddle boat on the first lake.

(Northampton Chronicle & Echo)

133. Very different weather conditions at ground level in Abington Park on Saturday 16 January 1960 as children flock to the Park with their toboggans and make the most of the recent snow-fall. The stone water-tower for so long a familiar landmark was constructed in 1678 to provide water for Abington Manor. *(Northampton Chronicle & Echo)*

134. (opposite) and 135. (above) All the fun of the fair at Northampton show in Abington Park during the early evening on Monday 1 August 1960 (opposite) and at night (above) on Friday 5 August 1966. For years, fairs have attracted youngsters with their bright multi-coloured lights and loud music, along with the chance of winning prizes on the sideshows and the excitement of the daredevil rides. In the early evening view (opposite) people stand on the perimeter of a stomach-churning ride waiting their turn to get on, as a representative of the older generation disembarks. In the incredible night-time view (above) the photographer has used a time exposure to capture the movement of the ride, the bright lights and the atmosphere of a fair after dark. *(Both pictures: Northampton Chronicle & Echo)*

136. A dramatic aerial view of a famous Northampton landmark photographed on Friday 27 July 1966 – the two huge cooling towers of the Power Station. The Northampton factory fortnight holiday is about to begin and with temperatures in the high 70s many local people have decided to visit the open air swimming pool at Midsummer Meadow and start their holiday early. The River Nene winds its way across the view, with Midsummer Meadow on the right linking up with Becket's Park, named after the nearby historic Becket's well, at the top of the picture. For centuries the Becket's Park area was known as Cow Meadow. The Avon cosmetics complex can be seen situated on the left beside the river. On the Bedford Road the United Counties garage can be seen near the bend in the road. *(Northampton Chronicle & Echo)*

137. Jumping for joy. Two girls enjoy their day at the open-air swimming pool at Midsummer Meadow on Saturday 8 August 1959. For years the pool provided enjoyment for Northamptonians. During the war, visiting troops would take a dip and, more recently, players from the Cobblers would train in the meadow and then have a swim. It was usually open between May and September, and on warm sunny days crowds would pack the area. The nearby Power Station provided a continuous flow of heated chlorinated water for the pool. In the early 1980s, local government cutbacks in expenditure meant that the pool closed, and it was finally demolished in 1983, much to the disappointment of many local people. Another sad loss for Northampton. (Northampton Chronicle & Echo)

138. Chipperfield's Circus comes to town! Crowds queue outside the elaborately decorated entrance to the Big Top under the gaze of the two huge cooling towers in Midsummer Meadow. That this is in the 1950s period is quite evident from the clothes people are wearing and the prams and pushchairs that are being pushed. *(Les Hanson)*

139. People sit out in the sun and enjoy a traction engine rally on land adjacent to Bedford Road on Saturday 7 May 1960. The steam propelled vehicles chug round the parade ring as judging takes place. The second vehicle, named 'Dorothy' is a steam lorry from Phipp's Northampton Brewery Company Ltd. The fluted sandstone chimney in the distance was built in 1862 to vent sewage purifying tanks then in use. As yet there are no signs of the Borough Council offices or any other buildings on the opposite side of Bedford Road. *(Northampton Chronicle & Echo)*

140. The carnival parade of 1963 was certainly one to remember as it was one of the biggest in the then 73 year history of Northampton's annual event. A record 290 entries and 120 lavishly decorated floats, with 2,500 people taking part, made its boisterous four-mile journey through the town on Thursday 20 June. It took an hour for all the entries to get on the road from a 7 p.m. departure from Midsummer Meadow, and it was nearly 10 p.m. before they all arrived safely at Abington Park. The photograph shows the parade winding its way up the Drapery with crowds of Northamptonians both sides of the road waiting to throw their contributions. The Carnival Queen float had been prepared by British Timken Ltd. and was escorted on its way by members of the Northampton Vespa Club on their gleaming machines. Two of this party can be seen. The Carnival Queen on this occasion was Rosemary Bodsworth, and she is with her Maids of Honour – Susan Wilson and Carol Bell. The total proceeds topped a then record figure of just under £1,600. *(Northampton Chronicle & Echo)*

141. A preserved steam roller, the pride of the Borough Engineers Department, chugs down St Giles Street on Thursday 17 June 1971, appearing in the Northampton Carnival for the first time. The 13-ton roller is an Allchin, built in 1899 and listed as 'No. 1' on the books of the Highways Department. At the time Mr Bert Henman, the plant engineer at the West Bridge depot, put a lot of time and effort into getting the old lady back into working order. With decimalization having taken place earlier in the year, many people used the carnival as an opportunity to offload their old pre-decimal coins but, even so, plenty of new coins were also thrown. On this occasion the carnival procession was 1¹/₂ miles in length and some 4,000 local people took part.

(Northampton Borough Council)

142. Northampton Art School students decided to advertise their forthcoming Arts Revel event in a unique fashion. They created a strange-looking monster and carried it around Northampton on Wednesday 5 December 1962. The picture shows them in Kettering Road, and their monster certainly surprised shoppers as it trotted around in the charge of its keeper who was wearing 'keeper's pads!   *(Northampton Chronicle & Echo)*

143. Students from Northampton Art School sit and stand on the steps outside All Saints Church on Saturday 11 June 1960 in their Annual Rag week activities to raise money for charity. With bloomers being the theme of this particular campaign, they are all joining in with the spirit of the occasion and have dressed up accordingly. *(Northampton Chronicle & Echo)*

144. At the Boughton cross roads on the Harborough Road just outside Northampton, two highwaymen (or ladies) wait in ambush on Tuesday 23 May 1967. Due shortly was a stagecoach, sponsored by a mustard manufacturer, making a 125th anniversary run of the last stagecoach service between York and London. The highwaymen (or ladies) were from rival mustard company, Taylors of Newport Pagnell, the right hand one being Mrs Susan Taylor, wife of the firm's managing director. Fortunately the police and stagecoach driver had been forewarned of the event, but the passengers and other people in the vicinity must have had quite a shock.

(Northampton Chronicle & Echo)

145. A view across part of the 70-acre Duston showground where the annual British Timken Show is being staged on Saturday 31 August 1963. A prestigious occasion with many events taking place in many different areas, ranging from flowers and vegetables to livestock. On this day the BBC TV cameras were present to broadcast the show-jumping event for the Olympic Trials. BBC radio was also there to present a programme for the first time from the show. Since the show had become a two-day event in 1949 it had been acknowledged as one of the best in the country. The standard had always been high and it had even been labelled as the best outside Chelsea. Few of those who staged the first British Timken Show in 1945 could have foreseen that the employees' flower show – which also incorporated a baby show, a children's pets competition and a one-man equestrian act – would grow into the two-day spectacular it became. The event attracted some 3,000 people in 1945, this number growing to 33,000 by 1959, but sadly the show was discontinued in 1978.

(Northampton Chronicle & Echo)

146. This intriguing aerial view was photographed on Tuesday 30 September 1947 from about 4,800 ft. It reveals an interesting picture of the 'borough's' area of the town between St Andrew's Road, running parallel to the railway and Horsemarket, Mayor Hold and St Andrew's Street on the right-hand side. The railway station area and many rows of sidings suggests busy times on the railway, and one of the freight trains stabled in the station has as many as 55 wagons being hauled by two steam engines. In the years to come, many of the streets were to disappear with modernization. *(Northampton Borough Council Archive)*

147. A nostalgic look back to the forecourt of Castle Station which will remind many local folk of their train journeys to and from Northampton. It is Friday 9 May 1964 and a hive of activity shows some of the group of 630 Northampton pensioners returning from a week's holiday at Southsea. The trip had been organized by the Northampton Old People's Voluntary Welfare Committee in the days when group train travel was commonplace.

(Northampton Chronicle & Echo)

148. (below) Holidaymakers gather by Wyman's bookstall on Platform 1 at Castle Station waiting for their special train to Hastings on Saturday 23 July 1960. The holiday exodus had begun on Friday afternoon, and up to 8 a.m. on the Saturday morning some 6,000 people had left Castle Station by train. All but two of the 12 special holiday trains (one to Yarmouth and one to Morecambe) were packed to the doors. The special services on the Saturday had made up the equivalent of a train more than a mile long to take Northampton people to holiday destinations all over the country. This shows how well used train travel was during the 1950s and 60s. It didn't take much persuasion to get away for holidays at the time, as up to 23 July 1960 it had been one of the wettest Julys on record in Northampton!

(Northampton Chronicle & Echo)

149. (above) A rare photograph taken inside the old refreshment room at Castle Station on Saturday 31 January 1959. A chance for passengers to come in from the cold and have a cup of tea or coffee and a currant bun before their journey. The old character of the station is still very much in evidence, with the decorative tiled floor and the basic but clean surroundings. On occasions, smoke from passing trains would enter the room and create a wonderful atmosphere only to be enjoyed in steam days. Somehow, to many railway enthusiasts, the refreshments always tasted better with the smell of steam and smoke in the vicinity!

(Northampton Chronicle & Echo)

150. Passenger traffic on the railways increased considerably at holiday times, requiring many extra trains to be fitted into the normal timetable. Here we see one such special easing its way through Castle Station on the centre road heading southwards behind Stanier Jubilee No. 45560 PRINCE EDWARD ISLAND at the end of July 1958. Passengers in the adjacent train turn their heads to glance at the Jubilee as they await their train's departure northwards from Platform 6.   *(C. Lucas)*

151. A splendid aerial view of the County Ground Northampton on Friday 22 July 1966 showing how the cricket club shared the ground with the football club. Cricket was first played on the ground in 1886, and the first football matches in 1897. Until the last football match took place in 1995 it was the only first-class cricket ground in the country to share with a professional league football club. In that 98 year period the largest football crowd to attend was in April 1966 when over 24,500 people crammed in to see the Cobblers play Fulham in a game that the Cobblers lost and consequently were relegated to Division II. The record crowd for a single day on the cricket side was that against the Australian cricket team in 1953 when a staggering 21,770 turned up to watch the game. As the cricket club owned the ground, during the summer months the football pitch was poorly treated, as illustrated on the photograph. In fact, part of the football pitch was used as a car park, with half the pitch being overlapped by the cricket boundary. At least the goalmouths were protected. In the picture Northants were playing Warwickshire and the game ended in a draw. The next game over the weekend was against the famous West Indies, which remarkably the home side won inside two days.
(Northampton Chronicle & Echo)

153. (below) It is the first Saturday home game of the new season at the County Ground, and for the first time in the Club's history they are in the First Division, and Manchester United are due on this 28 August 1965. Just hours before the kick-off, final preparations are in hand, and three young supporters look at the Cobblers coat of arms which is in the process of being fixed above the Directors Entrance in Abington Avenue. At the time there was great anticipation of what was to come, and it is a period that will be long remembered by the many fans who supported the Cobblers during that unique season. *(Northampton Chronicle & Echo)*

152. (above) The summer break is over for the Cobblers players, and it is back to training for the new season. Outside the County Ground, Dave Bowen (far left) leads his players for a training run on Monday 20 July 1959 at the start of his first season as manager of the Club. Dave Bowen, who lived in Northampton, played for the Cobblers during the 1947-50 period before going to Arsenal for nine years where he captained the side as well as winning 19 Welsh caps. He took the team on a meteoric rise from the fourth to the first division in six years, and then took over the duties of general manager/secretary in 1967. He later returned to manage the side again in 1969. He also managed the Welsh side for a period from 1964. Another player worthy of note in the photograph is Tommy 'Flash' Fowler, who is just behind the Cobblers' goalkeeper, Tony Brewer, who is wearing a tracksuit. Tommy Fowler played 564 games for the Cobblers and scored 90 goals, a record that is unlikely to be equalled, and a player that will be long remembered by local football fans. *(Northampton Chronicle & Echo)*

154. A typical view of the famous 'Hotel End' at the County Ground, packed with Cobblers supporters both young and old. On this occasion on Saturday 19 October 1963 the Cobblers are to play Charlton Athletic in a Division II game. On the day 15,221 fans turned out to see the Cobblers lose 2–1 in a game in which they missed chance after chance to win. No doubt many of the fans in the photograph were regular 'Hotel Enders', and the following season was to see them rewarded with the team being promoted to Division I. *(Northampton Chronicle & Echo)*

155. To compare with the picture opposite, this is a view of the other end of the pitch at the County Ground – the 'Spion Kop'. Once again, a very big crowd has gathered to watch the game on Saturday 9 October 1965 when the Cobblers play Sheffield United. At that part of the season Sheffield were flying high and came to the County Ground topping the First Division table. The Cobblers, alas, were next but one from the bottom. The game ended with a 1–0 win for the United side. The next home game for the Cobblers was against West Ham at which they finally recorded their first win in Division I. *(Northampton Chronicle & Echo)*

156. Pre-match entertainment from the 'King Bees' at the Cobblers versus Coventry local derby game on a cold Saturday 23 January 1965. With the ground filling up and the programme seller making his way around the perimeter of the pitch, the group play their music for an hour as rival groups of supporters gradually make themselves heard. The match ended as a 1–1 draw, and the Cobblers fans went home wondering how it was that the superior home side had not won. It was the first time that a rock group had played at the County Ground, and one wonders what Jimmy Hill, the Coventry manager must have thought of it. *(Northampton Chronicle & Echo)*

157. (right) One of the 7th Parachute Regiment Royal Horse Artillery helicopters suddenly arrives, causing a stir on the pitch as practice balls are thrown down to the players minutes before the start of the Cobblers Third Division game with Reading on Saturday 9 September 1967. Another game in which the home team nonchalantly threw away two silly goals and, although they scored through Frank Large, lost the game 2–1. The following season the downward trend continued and the Cobblers were back in Division 4 in 1969 after nine years absence! *(Northampton Chronicle & Echo)*

158. (below) A day to remember at the County Ground on Saturday 27 February 1960 when the Cobblers had an 8–1 victory over Oldham Athletic in the Fourth Division. One of the eight goals that hit the back of the net can be seen on its way into the net in this excellent action shot. In the background is the stand in its entirety before being rebuilt following the tragic fire at the Bradford City football ground.
(Northampton Chronicle & Echo)

159. The Australian cricket team have arrived in town and it is Saturday 27 June 1964, the first day's play against Northamptonshire at the County Ground. Colin 'Ollie' Milburn, the county's opening batsman, hits out in his usual exciting style. On this occasion he scored 27 runs before the end of his innings 'leg before wicket'. He was one of the biggest crowd-pullers and most popular figures at the County Ground during his career which was tragically cut short by a road accident in which he lost his left eye. He made his Test debut at Old Trafford against the West Indies in 1966, and his last century for England came on the 1969 winter tour in Pakistan. Over 13,500 spectators watched the Australians over the three days and the game ended in a draw. *(Northampton Chronicle & Echo)*

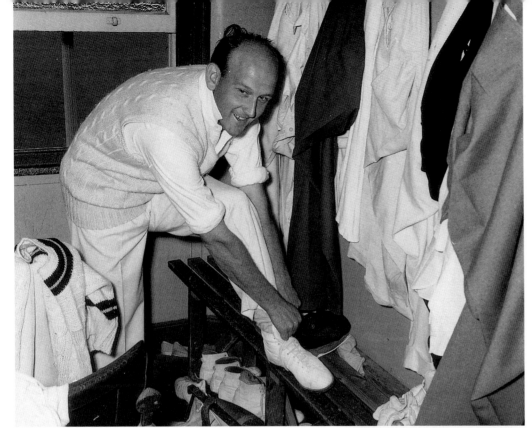

160. (left) Northamptonshire cricket history was made in 1954 when both fast bowler Frank Tyson and wicketkeeper Keith Andrew were chosen for the England touring team of Australia. Earlier that summer Frank Tyson played his first Test match against Pakistan. He was to become a national hero as the world's fastest bowler, earning him the nickname of 'Typhoon Tyson'. In Melbourne during the 1954-55 series, his seven wickets for 27 runs in Australia's second innings ensured an English win by 128 runs. He played in 14 Test matches, took a total of 46 wickets, and will long be remembered. The photograph shows him on 19 August 1960 at the County Ground towards the end of his career. *(Northampton Chronicle & Echo)*

161. (right) With rain pouring down at the County Ground on Wednesday 31 July 1968, play between Northamptonshire and Nottinghamshire is completely washed out, restricting the game to two days. Northamptonshire's batsman Colin Milburn (left) and team captain Roger Prideaux (right) find time to talk to Nottinghamshire's captain Gary Sobers, probably the finest all-rounder in the world. Roger Prideaux made his Test debut for England in 1968 against Australia in the fourth Test at Headingley. In the 1966 season he scored almost 2,000 runs. Gary Sobers had previously played at the County Ground two seasons earlier when Northamptonshire beat the West Indies in two days! Play finally got under way and the home team won the match. *(Northampton Chronicle & Echo)*

162. Part of the crowd in the main stand at the Franklin's Gardens ground, home of Northampton rugby, settling down to watch a game on Saturday 26 October 1963. The Tigers from Leicester are the opponents, and on this occasion the Saints lost by 11 points to nil! It was Leicester's first win at Franklin's Gardens for six years, and their biggest victory there since the 1929-30 season. Generally, though, the Saints were a top rugby club in England during the 1960s, and with a team of international-class players they did not get nearly enough support compared to the crowds that visited the County Ground.

(Northampton Chronicle & Echo)

163. (above) Photographed on Saturday 14 March 1959 before the match with Rosslyn Park, the picture shows Saints centre-threequarter Jeff Butterfield receiving an inscribed silver salver from Saints President Mr G.S. Sturtridge. The silver salver was in recognition of Jeff becoming the first Northampton player to captain an England rugby team. *(Northampton Chronicle & Echo)*

164. (below) The visit to Franklin's Gardens of local rugby rivals Leicester has over the years produced some very exciting games. Here the teams are in action on Saturday 28 February 1959. On this day, although the Saints were behind at the interval, and a man short, they rallied and ran out winners by 22 points to 13. Not only was it the double over the Tigers for the season, but it was the highest number of points the Saints had ever scored against them. The Saints at this time were England's top club. *(Northampton Chronicle & Echo)*

165. An aerial view of Billing Aquadrome on Friday 22 July 1966 situated, at the time, some distance from Northampton town boundary and still looked upon as a trip into the county. Even in 1966 the rows of caravans are evident, although the numbers would greatly increase over the years. Also in view is the swimming pool which would regularly be packed out on sunny days, especially during the holiday period.

(Northampton Chronicle & Echo)

166. It is Whit Monday 30 May 1966 and for once the weather is warm and sunny – perfect conditions to be out and about. By the amazing number of people who are enjoying themselves at the Billing Aquadrome swimming pool, it appears that many Northamptonians were making sure of a 'dip' during the day. In fact, attendances were at record levels on both the Sunday and Monday of that holiday weekend. Can you recognize yourself amongst the many faces?

(Northampton Chronicle & Echo)

167. Lazy and very enjoyable summer days could be spent in the beautiful surroundings of Overstone Solarium swimming pool, as shown in this photograph taken on Bank Holiday Monday 28 August 1967, although on this occasion space seems to be very much at a premium around the perimeter of the pool with people sunbathing, but not that many are actually taking the plunge.

(Northampton Chronicle & Echo)

168. Another pleasant out of town venue for lazing about and swimming was Wilby Lido, although it was to close in the early 1960s. In this picture, taken on Tuesday 2 August 1960, a young lady takes up the classic 'sensual model' pose for her boyfriend to photograph her, although the *Chronicle & Echo* photographer no doubt ended up taking the better picture.

(Northampton Chronicle & Echo)

169. They say that seeing is believing, and on Monday 16 August 1965 at Billing Aquadrome people gazed in amazement as a car drove down the slipway into the water and proceeded to cross the lake – an instant metamorphosis from car to boat. It was, in fact, an amphibious Amphicar belonging to Mr Jim Robinson of Boughton Mill, and could be bought for the princely sum of £1,100 on the road (or water). Powered by a Triumph Herald engine with separate transmission to wheels and twin nylon screws, which could be engaged separately, or together for when entering or leaving the water, the Amphicar had a top speed of 75 m.p.h. on the road and 7.5 knots in the water. Another unusual feature for a boat was that the front wheels acted as a rudder.

(Northampton Chronicle & Echo)

170. Another vehicle in the water – this time because of flooding. A United Counties Leyland double-decker bus, without the benefit of twin nylon screws (see previous picture), heads for Northampton on Monday 5 December 1960 along the Cogenhoe to Northampton Road near Billing Aquadrome during a spell of particularly wet weather.

(Northampton Chronicle & Echo)

171. The photographer has captured an idyllic scene in the woods at Billing Aquadrome on Saturday 23 March 1957. There is a real feeling of spring in the air as the sun streams down on the two ladies gathering daffodils to brighten their homes as winter comes to an end for another year.

(Northampton Chronicle & Echo)

172. A popular attraction at Billing Aquadrome used to be the Aqua-Belle which provided trips around the lake. The boat is seen here as it sails through a patch of sunlight on Whit Monday 18 May 1959 loaded to capacity. Aqua-Belle would provide many more pleasurable cruises before retirement in the 1970s. *(Northampton Chronicle & Echo)*

173. (left) A busy scene at the north end of Blisworth tunnel in the mid-1920s as the Grand Junction Canal Company's steam tug 'Anslow' arrives with the 2 p.m. trip from Stoke Bruerne. It is pulling through an as yet unseen pair of boats, for which the horses on the towpath are waiting, having been brought over the top of the tunnel. Waiting to go south are a pair of mill boats carrying coal for John Dickinson's paper mills at Croxley, near Watford. They will be pulled through the tunnel by 'Anslow' on the return trip at 3.30 p.m.

(*L.J. Thompson*)

174. (right) In the same location as the picture above on a summer's day in the 1930s, a pair of Fellows Morton and Clayton boats make good headway, probably carrying groceries from London to Birmingham. At this time the canal was still in competition with the London Midland and Scottish railway for carrying goods, and by the wake the boat is creating, its 15 hp Bolinder semi-diesel engine is working hard pulling the unpowered 'butty' boat just emerging from the tunnel.

(*L.J. Thompson*)

REC. AT LOUGHBOROUGH. No 64.

175. A peaceful scene at Blisworth Mill on Tuesday 2 June 1959 as a boy proudly wearing a 'Davy Crockett' hat brings his budgerigar up from below for a breath of fresh air. At this time the boats bound for the Northampton Arm and Wellingborough were being unloaded at Blisworth and the goods taken by road owing to lock damage on the Rothersthorpe flight during the construction of the M1 motorway. *(Northampton Chronicle & Echo)*

176. British Waterways boats, loaded with coal for Dickinson's paper mills at Croxley, thread their way through Blisworth tunnel as they approach the southern end on Tuesday 30 December 1958. Blisworth tunnel is 3,076 yards long and straight, and takes approximately 30 minutes to pass through. In the days of the steam tugs, the boiler required re-firing on the way through, coating the roof in a thick layer of soot. Between 1980 and 1984 the tunnel was closed, and during this time major structural repairs were carried out to the centre section. *(Northampton Chronicle & Echo)*

177. Boat children stroll along the towpath as a pair of narrow boats belonging to Samuel Barlow Coal Co. Ltd. pass under the bridge at Whilton Locks loaded with coal, heading for Kearley and Tonges jam factory at Southall on Saturday 11 April 1959. These narrow boats travelled in pairs, only one being powered, in this case No. 54 'Neptune' with the rudder. The unpowered boat, known as the 'butty' boat, is seen here lashed alongside with rope fore and aft. Smoke drifts out from the galley in the butty boat as the stove is stoked up. *(Northampton Chronicle & Echo)*

178. A pair of British Waterways boats swing into the Northampton Arm of the Grand Union Canal on Thursday 30 April 1959 loaded with grain for Whitworth's Victoria Mills at Wellingborough, a practice that would continue for another 10 years. The building on the right was originally Pickford's warehouse and wharf before being taken over by the Grand Junction Canal Company when the branch to Northampton opened in May 1815, the building being demolished in the 1960s.

(Northampton Chronicle & Echo)

179. An unusual scene on the River Nene at Whitworths' Victoria Mills in Wellingborough on Thursday 1 September 1966 as the owner of 'Blue Dolphin' inspects the boat's moorings. The boats had been marooned since the river festival by floods which caused the water to spill over on to the adjacent path where the Rover and the boat owner are standing.

(Northampton Chronicle & Echo)

180. For the people of Northampton interested in railways during the days of the steam locomotive, a trip out to the Midland main line at Wellingborough made a change from the more familiar West Coast main line at Blisworth. Easter Saturday 1959 was not a good day to choose, however, as the rain lashed down at Wellingborough Midland Road Station. The porter looks out from under the canopy as Stanier Jubilee No. 45694 BELLEROPHON sounds its whistle at the photographer to get back from the platform edge as she sweeps through with a St Pancras bound express. *(Dave Rowe)*

181. Another scene at Wellingborough Midland Road Station, in much better weather conditions than the previous photograph, in the late afternoon of 26 December 1960. A glance over Mill Road bridge finds rebuilt Royal Scot No. 46118 ROYAL WELCH FUSILIER starting away from its Wellingborough stop with the Boxing Day express from St Pancras to Manchester. From a photographic point of view the lighting conditions were ideal, as the low winter sunshine reflects dramatically off the side of the train to produce a highly evocative image. *(P.H. Groom)*

183. (above) Streamlined Pacific No. 6225 DUCHESS OF GLOUCESTER leaves a trail of exhaust in the crisp evening air at Gayton Loops in February 1939. The white background of the 'Royal Scot' carriage boards together with the highly polished crimson and gold striped Duchess reflect the setting sun as she sweeps on towards Blisworth and her 5.25 p.m. Euston arrival time. *(W.J.S. Meredith)*

182. (left) Many people travelled from Northampton to Blisworth in order to have a picnic with their children in the fields adjacent to Gayton loops whilst watching the trains go by on the West Coast main line. Here in the summer of 1952 Stanier 8F No. 48486 waits in the loop with its guard's van by the London and North Western signals, affectionately known as 'Big Ben' and 'Little Len'. In the field a boy finds something more interesting to look at through his telescope further down the field. *(P.I. Rawlinson)*

184. It was worth taking a trip to the main line for a glimpse of the new streamlined 'Coronation Scot' service when it was introduced in 1937. The train received a lot of publicity when on its first test run it broke the existing speed record, reaching 114 m.p.h. The blue and silver stripes on the locomotive continued along the coaches for the whole length of the train, and this impressive sight is seen here racing northwards through the Northamptonshire countryside near Bugbrooke, hauled by streamlined Pacific No. 6222 QUEEN MARY during Easter 1938.

(J. Davis)

185. (above) and 186. (opposite) For motor cycling enthusiasts the annual Boxing Day visit to Tunnel Hill Farm, Blisworth, is very much part of a tradition whatever the weather. For many years the Northampton Motor Cyclists Club has organized a motor bike scramble locally known as the 'Wild and Woolly' scramble. Invariably the weather at the end of December is wet and the course at Blisworth becomes extremely muddy, thus adding to the excitement of thrills and spills for the visiting spectators.

The picture above shows the scene in 1959 with the bikes sending up a massive spray of muddy water as they are ridden around the 20-lap course. On this occasion only 12 of the 41 starters completed the course. Opposite is a spectacular flash photograph taken at the event in 1958. The course is as muddy as ever, and rider No. 10 skilfully guns his Matchless up a slippery slope amidst a cloud of spray.

(Both pictures: Northampton Chronicle & Echo)

The first post-war British and European Grand Prix was given the name 'Grand Prix d'Europe' and was important enough to be made a Royal occasion at the Silverstone circuit on Saturday 13 May 1950.

187. (left) Their Majesties King George VI and Queen Elizabeth, and HRH Princess Margaret are received by civic dignitaries on their arrival at Brackley LNWR station prior to the short journey by car to the Silverstone circuit. *(Northampton Chronicle & Echo)*

188. (below) Teams busy themselves preparing the cars for the race on the Saturday. On the front row are two of the four Alfa Romeo 158s in the race. This was the first appearance of an Alfa Romeo Grand Prix team on British soil, and with Ferraris not running, they made a clean sweep to finish first, second and third more than two laps ahead of the field, driven by G. Farina, L. Fagioli and Reg Parnell (guest British driver) respectively. The fourth Alfa, driven by J.M. Fangio, retired. *(Northampton Chronicle & Echo)*

189. (above) Silverstone circuit has been used for various types of events over the years, and on Saturday 23 July 1960 it was the venue for the Vintage Sports Car Club meeting. The two big cars nearest the camera are a 1912 9,000 cc Mercedes (G2), and a 1908 12,000 cc Grand Prix Itala.
(Northampton Chronicle & Echo)

190. (below) Another event at Silverstone – this time the annual *Motor Cycling* and British Motor Cycling Club's International meeting on Saturday 18 April 1959. The photograph shows the riders on the grid lined up on the day before ready to practice for the 350 cc championship event.
(Northampton Chronicle & Echo)

191. People mill around the pits during a practice session for the British Grand Prix at Silverstone on Friday 18 July 1958 as Stirling Moss and Mike Hawthorn discuss the finer points of the Ferrari. In the race itself on the Saturday, Stirling Moss retired on the 26th lap in his Vanwall when lying second. Mike Hawthorn, driving a Ferrari, finished second to his team-mate Peter Collins. At the German Grand Prix the following month Peter Collins was fatally injured, and at the end of the season Mike Hawthorn became the first British World Champion. He retired while at the top of his profession, only to die in an accident in his Jaguar on the Guildford by-pass on Thursday 22 January 1959. *(Northampton Chronicle & Echo)*

192. (above) Although Graham Hill never managed to win the British Grand Prix, his son Damon achieved it on Sunday 10 July 1994, and is seen here on the podium waiting to receive his trophy from HRH Princess of Wales. Dad would have been proud.
(Northampton Chronicle & Echo)

193. (right) Formula 1 champion Graham Hill, seen here clutching a bottle of Fanta and talking to an up-and-coming Jackie Stewart before the qualifying session at Silverstone on Saturday 10 July 1965. Both these men were exceptional Formula 1 drivers, winning a total of five World Championships between them.
(Northampton Chronicle & Echo)

194. When Go-Kart racing was first introduced it became a very popular sport mainly because it was not that difficult to build your own machine and at a price that most people could afford. Here at Earls Barton on Saturday 30 July 1960 the starter hurries off the track as a race gets under way at the old dog-racing stadium. *(Northampton Chronicle & Echo)*

195. On a day out to Sywell Aerodrome, part of a crowd of 5,000 gaze skywards as three Tiger Moths drone overhead forming part of an air display on Whit Monday 7 June 1965. In all 18 Tiger Moths took part in the aerobatic display piloted by men and women of the Tiger Club. There was also a demonstration of parachute jumping.

(Northampton Chronicle & Echo)

196. A young racegoer enjoys the sunshine while sitting amongst the runners and riders (metaphorically speaking) at Towcester racecourse on Whit Monday 7 June 1965.

(Northampton Chronicle & Echo)

197. Could this be a racecourse or a circus, or both! While the bookmaker counts his takings, a section of the crowd perform a wonderful balancing act in front of the grandstand as everyone's eyes are on the final furlong to see if their fancied horse has any chance of winning. The performance is at the Towcester National Hunt meeting on Saturday 28 May 1966.

(Northampton Chronicle & Echo)

198. Against a backdrop of typical Northamptonshire countryside, runners are led round the parade ring at Towcester racecourse before the first race of the day on Saturday 28 May 1966. With the sun streaming down, the crowds were out in force in this most pleasurable of surroundings. Racing began at Towcester in the 1870s when the Empress of Austria organized the first meeting when staying at the stately mansion of the Hesketh family at Easton Neston. *(Northampton Chronicle & Echo)*

199. A scene from the stands at the Northampton Agricultural Society's County Show at Overstone Park on Saturday 14 September 1957. The glorious summer weather has brought people out in vast numbers to this attractive venue where they crowd round to get a better view of the goings on in an equally crowded show ring. The last ever County Show was held in the pouring rain at Overstone Park in 1971.

(Northampton Chronicle & Echo)

200. Mr Joe Wright heads the Woodland Pytchley Hunt through typical woodland near Southwick on Easter Monday 13 April 1959; an environment that called for strong horses and bold riders and only the most dedicated of hunt followers. *(Northampton Chronicle & Echo)*

INDEX

201. Two models pose for two cameras at Billing Aquadrome on Thursday 24 January 1967. The model underneath is an Aston Martin DB6, the model on top was probably frozen.

(Northampton Chronicle & Echo)

An aerial panorama looking over Spencer bridge and the railway marshalling yards towards Kings Heath during the late summer of 1963. *(Northampton Borough Council Archive)*